Kay Kerr is an autistic author and journalist hoping to shift perspectives on autism and neurodiversity through her writing. Her debut novel *Please Don't Hug Me* (2020) was shortlisted for Book of the Year for Older Children at the Australian Book Industry Awards (ABIA) in 2021, and listed as a 'Notable Book' by the Children's Book Council of Australia (CBCA). Her second novel *Social Queue* (October 2021) was also a CBCA 'Notable Book', and was shortlisted for the Queensland Literary Awards.

Through her freelance work, Kay writes about autistic representation, disability, parenting, pop culture, gardening and feelings.

She lives on the Sunshine Coast, Queensland, with her husband and daughter.

Also by Kay Kerr
Please Don't Hug Me
Social Queue

KAY KERR

LOVE & AUTISM

MACMILLAN

Pan Macmillan Australia

Pan Macmillan acknowledges the Traditional Custodians of country throughout Australia and their connections to lands, waters and communities. We pay our respect to Elders past and present and extend that respect to all Aboriginal and Torres Strait Islander peoples today. We honour more than sixty thousand years of storytelling, art and culture.

Some of the people in this book have had their names changed to protect their identities.

First published 2023 in Macmillan by Pan Macmillan Australia Pty Ltd
1 Market Street, Sydney, New South Wales, Australia, 2000

A catalogue record for this book is available from the National Library of Australia

Typeset in 12.5pt Adobe Garamond Pro by Midland Typesetters, Australia

Printed by IVE

Any health or medical content contained in this book is not intended as health or medical advice. The publishers and their respective employees, agents and authors are not liable for injuries or damage occasioned to any person as a result of reading or following any health or medical content contained in this book.

The author and the publisher have made every effort to contact copyright holders for material used in this book. Any person or organisation that may have been overlooked should contact the publisher.

The paper in this book is FSC® certified. FSC® promotes environmentally responsible, socially beneficial and economically viable management of the world's forests.

For the autistic community, with love and gratitude

CONTENTS

LOVE
&
AUTISM

A SNAPPY INTRODUCTION

The best thing about my first kiss was that it happened in another country. It was simple – I met a boy I thought was cute, and he thought my strangeness was due to my being Australian, which, for reasons I believe were linked strongly to the popularity of *Home and Away* at the time, led to a brief romantic interlude on a holiday that was otherwise populated entirely by relatives. And then I hopped on a plane, flew 15,000 kilometres home, and never saw him again.

The kiss itself I can't really remember, and prosopagnosia (the inability to recognise faces) means I definitely don't remember his face, but I do recall the aftermath. In a valiant effort to 'holiday up' a trip to visit my grandfather in Ireland after his double-bypass heart surgery, my mother took me and my two brothers to London on the way home. We crammed into the one-bedroom apartment of a family friend for a few nights, went to see *The Lion King* in West End, caught double-decker buses, visited the weird wax museum, ate a lot of McDonald's, and saw the bridges and churches and towers. I was miserable the entire time, in a way only a fourteen-year-old on a budget-stretching family holiday of a lifetime could be. I remember moping around the city, lugging my Discman to all the tea towel landmarks and listening to the CD single of a British *Pop Idol* runner-up on repeat. The same song again and again and again; no surprises there. Nothing impressed me, not the London Eye, not the pickle building, and definitely not the guards doing their little march out the front of Buckingham Palace. I returned home changed, matured and age-appropriately melancholic.

No romantic endeavour, successful or otherwise, has ever been that easy again. I understood that first kiss because it involved very little subtext. There was no room for confusion, or for mistakes. It was what it was, and there was nothing I could have done that would have led to a different ending. I appreciate it for its clarity, if nothing else.

●

Okay, now that I have shared a funny anecdote about my first foray into the world of love and romance, let's talk about the other part of this book's title: autism. Autism is an invisible disability with a long and complex history. Parents were once blamed for their children's autism – 'refrigerator mothers' and the like – and so autism was framed as an awful thing that could happen to your child, and it was your fault if it did. Echoes of those attitudes still exist today; you do not have to look far for examples. Suffice to say that to be autistic is to become well-acquainted with 'deficit'. We are identified by deficits, measured on deficits, compared by deficits and treated for our deficits. Even before I knew I was autistic, I felt those perceived deficits. Diagnosis does not dispel them. If anything, it has the possibility of affirming them, if diagnosis is all you have, without support or community. That is in no small part due to the language and framing of autism itself. It is all laid out in the fifth edition of the *Diagnostic and Statistical Manual of Mental Disorders* (*DSM-5*), which is the standard text used to diagnose autism in Australia and many other parts of the world. The criteria demand 'persistent deficits in social communication and social interaction across multiple contexts'. I mean, sure, but by whose standards? What I once accepted as fact I grow to question more and more. Explorations of love and autism (see what I did there?) tend to focus on what the autistic person is lacking, and what they must overcome, but that is not what this book is about. This is a closer look at some autistic lives and a celebration of what autistic people bring to their relationships – not despite being autistic, but because of it.

If you do not yet have the pleasure of knowing an autistic person, may these stories fill that space in your life. If you do have that pleasure, or you are that pleasure, I hope these stories of love fill your heart. The five people I have been lucky enough to include in these pages – Michael, Jess, Noor, Tim and Chloë – have gifted me, and you as readers, with so much.

Michael, who many know as a breakout star of ABC TV's *Love on the Spectrum,* charmed the world with his quest to find a romantic partner. Now in his late twenties, Michael is carving out a life of abundance with his steadfast commitment to being his authentic self. During our talks, we delved into his early childhood days, his close-knit and quirky family, the hard parts of growing up 'almost normal', and the new path he is now on, shooting for the stars.

Jess is one of the first autistic friends I made when I was diagnosed, and I have learned so much from her. Like me, Jess is in her thirties, but unlike me she received her diagnosis as a child. Through our interviews, I discovered that what I thought would have made the journey easier actually came with a whole different set of challenges. Her hard-won triumph is the life she has created for herself that is entirely her own.

I came to know Noor through her writing. I reached out in a fangirl kind of way, and I have been rewarded with conversations of immense richness and beauty. The way she shines a light on her own experiences and her 'fragmented life' – which includes her culture, her religion, her life as a young migrant and the balancing act required to straddle all those roles – is stunning. Noor shares her story under a pseudonym.

Tim is a young advocate whose work I came across through Victorian autism organisation Amaze. He is non-speaking and uses an augmentative and alternative communication method known as partner-assisted typing (PAT). Tim and his mum Sarah have navigated systems that are not always accommodating of those with complex and high support needs, and Tim's story is a testament to the love between mother and son.

Chloë has the kind of self-awareness and wider understanding of autistic history and culture that I only wish I had at her age. Our chats were eye-opening and full of joy. She looks at love not through the neurotypical lens of what is expected of us by society, but by considering what feels good and right for her. Hers is a beautiful, butterflies-in-your-stomach kind of story, but not without its own peaks and troughs.

My interview style has been a gentle one. I would never want anyone to share more of their story than they are truly comfortable with. This means that some of the stories are longer than others, and some go into more detail in certain areas. This is purposeful, as I did not wish to fictionalise any elements either. As well as the stories of Michael, Jess, Noor, Tim and Chloë, I include many other autistic voices. More is more, I believe. Yes, I am a journalist, but this isn't a book about the research. There are already several wonderful books by better researchers than me. (See my recommended reading list for a starting point.) My background is as a community journalist, so this is a book about people. The best thing about being autistic is the people. My brain adores patterns, finding them in the way I imagine neurotypical people might find something inconsequential to add to a light conversation: with ease. As I pored over the notes from my interviews, the patterns started to emerge. The stories are all so different, but familiar too. Across these five distinct lives I could see similar through-lines and themes, moments and questions. I looked at my own experiences, and those of the dozens of other people I spoke to, and I wrote all that I could see. I never grow tired of talking to autistic people about their lives. To diverge from what is typical is to develop interesting perspectives, unique ideas and new ways of thinking. I want to hear them all.

•

I don't know what brings you to this book. Maybe you are an autistic person who feels pride in your identity. Maybe you have been taught to feel shame around the things you do differently or the areas where you need support. Maybe you are a family member or friend of an autistic person, nodding along in recognition or wanting to know more. Maybe you work with autistic people through your job, or maybe you have and just never realised it. Maybe your understanding of autism comes primarily from the movie *Rain Man* and TV's Sheldon Cooper. Maybe you think 'there was none of this autism business around when I was young', and you are sceptical of the whole thing. It doesn't really matter. These stories are for everyone, and what you take from them is up to you.

I am an autistic woman, a writer, someone who has worked with autistic people in classrooms and support organisations, who is related to autistic people, friends with autistic people, who has an autistic child. I have felt both pride and shame. These days, it is mostly pride. I am also someone who didn't have any of this autism stuff around when I was a kid. I learned I am autistic when I was in my twenties. I am still learning. I love love. I am in love. I am undoing the idea that there is one 'right' way to do it. I still read and watch romance stories like it is my job. And, I suppose, in writing this book, it kind of is.

But this is not about me. This book started as me standing on tippy-toes, peeking over the wall, wondering what it is like for other people with brains like mine. What do their friendships look like, their families, their partners and their parenting? Love comes in many shapes and sizes, and I want to know about it all. I understand that romantic love is often seen as the pinnacle, the one thing to strive for above all else, but love is a gift in any form. A best friend can be a soulmate, and some of the strongest bonds I have ever witnessed have been between parent and child, and siblings, and chosen family who show up for one another in myriad ways every single day.

Some people have kindly invited me over the wall, and it is a great privilege to bear witness and share their stories. Because I know my circumstances have allowed me thus far to be the shiny, easily digestible autistic – the smiling white face and simple 'overcoming adversity' story, quick to translate into a short media bio or interview. I am conscious of the parts I hide – or don't hide, but choose not to illuminate. Like the anger, or the fact that my family eats the same meal five times a week because food is a struggle and that is where I let the plates drop. People around me prop me up so I look like I am doing all of this on my own. INDEPENDENTLY. I hate that word. I am not independent. I am not sure I know anyone who is truly independent, and I wonder why the concept is so highly valued. Community and acceptance seem much more worthy. I do not want to be the 'acceptable autistic'; I want us all to be accepted. I want to widen the scope of what people understand autism to be. I cannot speak from a place of knowing. I am an authority on nothing, least of all my own life. But I can share the questions on my mind and the curiosity I feel about the lives of other people.

So, this is not about me. This is about the people kind enough to share their stories, brave enough to put themselves out there, and strong enough to live their authentic lives in a world that often measures them by what they cannot do. Thank you Michael, Jess, Noor, Tim and Chloë. I hope that by telling these stories of autistic lives and loves, I will be sharing them through the lens with which I see them: not as other, but as kin.

THIS BIT *IS* ABOUT ME

Hello there, me again. As you have no doubt gathered by now, I am Kay and I am an autistic writer. I have always been autistic, and, bar a couple of years at the start there, I suppose I have always been a writer as well. Or, more accurately, I have always been obsessed with stories. And books. Books, books, glorious books. Books don't call you poor for having the wrong sneakers on sports day, and books would never dump you over MSN Messenger right before you have to start a shift at McDonald's, forcing you to spend four hours mixing entirely too many McFlurrys and serving them with tears streaming down your face. No, books are the best. And the best books, to me, are the ones that explore ideas around or teach me something about love.

Love has always intrigued me, in part because I have carried for a long time a feeling that I am doing love wrong. I am not emotional enough in the ways people expect, and too emotional in ways they do not like to see. My tears come too late, and never for the right reasons. The McFlurry tears weren't even about the boy; they were born of sheer frustration at having a choice (to be in a teen relationship or not) taken out of my hands. Knowing how things are going to go has always been important – too important, some would say. I don't ask the right questions or care about the right things. I don't thank people as much as they seem to want to be thanked. I like to be alone a lot more than other people, and I need things to be a certain way. How I feel in the moment is so big it often convinces me this is how I will feel forever. And that goes for all kinds of love. I have felt like the wrong kind of daughter, the wrong kind of sister and the wrong kind of friend. My mouth and my moods have got me in all kinds of trouble. Sensory processing distress can present as anger, and a meltdown can look a lot like rage. My direct communication style has embarrassed my mother in precarious social situations, like when a set of my Enid Blyton books were returned full of scribbles.

'It's fine,' she assured them.

'It's definitely not,' I raged.

At a time and place where everything was a behaviour, and behaviour was everything, I am not quite sure how many of my parents' friendships I detonated.

To my older brother, I was the spoiled child who demanded the things I wanted and was often given them above him because it meant keeping the peace. Things like the chicken breast instead of the leg, the mini box of Fruit Loops from the variety pack at

Christmas and, in my teenage years, most of the parental attention, because I was not handling things well and he seemed to
be doing just fine. My younger brother was my playmate, my
dress-up doll and my favourite little person, but I observed from
social situations that it was more acceptable to torment younger
siblings, and so that was what I began to do. I can still picture his
face breaking when I made fun of his appearance right at a time
when those things matter most, and I feel as crushed by it now as
I did all those years ago. I dropped real friendships in favour of
the ones I thought I needed to have, and took far too many years
to figure out this is a very good way to find yourself all alone.

Most relationships have, at one stage or another, been similarly fraught. Well, similar in that they have been fraught – the
manifestations of which have been wholly original, I will give
them that. But the point is, the feedback I received on a loop
from childhood through to becoming a young adult was that,
nope, that is not how it is done. You are doing it wrong.

This propelled me to study love – in other people, in movies
and books and on television. I committed to it in an intense way
I can see now is typical of my not-typical brain. I absorbed the
lines and the gestures, the tropes and the endings. I repeated
the words, again and again. An interesting approach, you might
think, to something we are supposed to *feel* more than learn. But
it *is* learned, as those of us who struggle to get it right realise.

I can see with hindsight how I have tripped up, how I have
failed to follow 'the rules' and said and done some incomprehensible things. In a lot of ways, I was doing love wrong. This was
because I was intent on acting like a neurotypical person, and in

order to do that I needed to smother, bury, deny and hide my autistic tendencies and needs.

And the thing is, I never passed as 'normal' for long; not really. 'Sometimes the sound of electricity keeps me up at night,' is certainly a bold choice of conversation starter. It goes down about as well as trying to explain why I am pulling out of a commitment at the last minute because I have already allocated my social energy for the day. Or why I get so mad if I am in a car where two different conversations are happening around me at once. I cannot think of something that fills me with more rage. The one thing I will give myself credit for, though, is that I have tried. I have tried unbelievably hard. I spent years pretending I was not trying, while trying so hard and wearing myself out with both the trying and the hiding of the trying. Phew – exhausting. I put so much effort into what I thought I had to be for other people that I failed to figure out who I wanted to be for me.

For about twenty years, give or take, I floated so many of what I thought were my own weird little idiosyncrasies in conversations, hoping that someone else might respond with 'me too' rather than a strange look and a sudden need to go and get another drink. I was starting to feel like the person in the apocalypse movie who broadcasts a radio message every day and never gets a response.

Getting an autism diagnosis in my twenties gave me the channel to tune into. It gave me people, a community at the end of my world, and it gave me hope with a new place to begin. My autism diagnosis gave me a context through which to understand my seemingly random struggles. The knowledge felt revolutionary.

It still does. I was a journalist who knew the who, where, what (me, in the drawing room, with a meltdown) and finally discovered the how and why (sensory overload, autism).

My diagnosis did not come from nowhere. It was the inevitable endpoint of a lot of years spent careening towards burnout and breakdown. My life was unsustainable as it was, with my career workload, unfathomably busy weekends, and never a minute to stop, to rest, to process. And it was all cumulative, every week harder than the one before. I was Artax sinking slowly into the swamp. Without any real understanding of my own support needs, I dulled sensory input with alcohol, I pushed down my emotions as a way to try and avoid dealing with them, and I was not really present in the relationships that meant the most to me. Burnout was the moment when all of that stopped working – not that it had ever really worked. I could no longer work, sleep, socialise, or function as I did before. Diagnosis was the starting point for undoing some of that damage. Before I had the label 'autistic', there were many others I wore. Some given to me by other people, under their breath or to my face, and some I bestowed on myself through the worst kind of worth-eroding self-talk. Labels like sensitive, difficult, particular, snobby, rude, blunt, angry, emotional, dramatic, crazy and bad. I like autistic a lot more.

•

Autistic research psychologist Jac den Houting talks about the paradigm shift around autism and neurodiversity from the medical assumption that there is one 'right' way to be, and any other way of being is wrong and needs to be fixed, to the view of neurodiversity as part of the range of natural variation in human neurology. They say in their 2019 TED Talk, 'Just like biodiversity helps to sustain a healthy physical environment, neurodiversity can help to create a healthy and sustainable cognitive environment. There are no right or wrong brains, all forms of neurological development are equally valid, and equally valuable. All people are entitled to full and equal human rights, and to be treated with dignity and respect.'

To understand this, I needed to reframe my thinking. Reading, listening to, connecting with and talking to other autistic people about their lives and their experience of love has changed my life. Because love does not have to look like a well-behaved child, a large friendship group maintained since school, public displays of affection or the parent who turns up to all the after-school events. It *can* look like that, sure, but that is not the only way. What one person deems the 'right' way to love is ultimately subjective, and there are neuronormative expectations at every turn. Why are eye contact and 'I love you' considered *the* markers of love in Western culture? Why not look at all the other ways an autistic person might show their love, such as being comfortable enough to be their full selves, turning to you when they are struggling, sharing their interests and wanting to be near you? Other people's versions of showing love have not always felt like love to me. Forced hugs and 'you're fine', and talking about that person we both like in a way that makes me wonder how you talk about me when I leave the room. I see how the word 'autism' is used to strip the humanity of others, how a person becomes a walking autism, to be kept over there and treated with caution or scorn. I do not like it. I want to change it. This is my attempt to change it.

•

'You are not like my autistic child,' is something autistic adults might hear if they start to talk about their experiences, particularly in online spaces. For some, the rise of autistic voices advocating for themselves feels like a threat to a conversation they have become used to dominating. (I am looking at you, Senator Hollie Hughes.) It seems like a no-brainer – I do not find it strange that an adult does not show many similarities to a small child, and I do not know of many non-autistic adults who resemble non-autistic children. Through this book, you will see autistic children become autistic adults, and how different they are now from their childhood selves. People who say that one autistic person is not representative of another because of the many different ways autism can present are both right and wrong – but, more importantly, they are missing the point. To access support, of course there needs to be differentiation, although I do not believe any autistic person is at risk of being over-supported in our society. But to truly understand autism is something else entirely. It is not about how these traits look from the outside; it is not even about there being 'traits' or 'presentations' at all. A neurotype is not defined by how it looks to or impacts on other people. It is about how we feel and how we function from the inside. I cannot see the world any other way, but when I look at an emotionally dysregulated child with daily one-on-one supports, or a teenager struggling socially with the high school hierarchy, or a burnt-out adult who is just finding themselves after diagnosis, I see them all as points on the same plane. I see the shared experiences and feelings, not the differences in the ways these look to other people.

Of course autism is not going to present in the same ways for everyone. People have different backgrounds, cultures, upbringings, personalities and experiences. People are at different stages of their lives. Some people need more support than others; some need lifelong support and have other coexisting conditions. But we share a way of being, a way of processing, that unites us in more ways than it separates us. And anyway, people who see autism as a list of symptoms are missing out on the best part – knowing an autistic person.

•

Autistic people are often criticised (I could end the sentence there) for being selfish, or self-obsessed, or tuning out other people. I worried when writing this that sharing snippets of my own story would be read as taking the spotlight away from the stories included in these pages. But I have come to understand that both the form and content of this book are autistic in nature. It is natural for me to think, and write, in tangential, associative ways. When people share their stories – gift me with their vulnerability and their open hearts – my brain rushes to bring forward the experiences of my own that match in theme or emotion. What other people often hear is 'now let me make this about me', but what I mean is 'you are not alone'. Because you really aren't. I promise.

LANGUAGE EXPLAINER

Given that this book is about the lives and stories of other people, the language used throughout reflects that. I respect that everyone has the right to identify and self-describe however they wish, and my aim is to be inclusive. I am also context-ualising language choices throughout the book with as much historical, cultural and political context as I can. Language is one part of the conversation around autism and neurodivergence, and it is ever-evolving.

In my writing, and in speaking about myself, I choose identity-first language (I am autistic) rather than person-first language (I am a person with autism). That is my preference, as I view being autistic as an intrinsic element to my identity in similar ways to gender, race and sexuality. This is the preference for many people in the autistic community, but not for all. I know that professionals who work with autistic people are often taught to use person-first language, because it separates the person from their condition. However, I do not think we need to separate autism from the person to be able to see and appreciate their humanity. Autism is not something I carry around with me, like sunglasses or a miniature poodle. It is part of my make-up, and it cannot be separated.

In general, I now try to avoid referring to autism spectrum disorder (ASD) as much as possible, as I do not believe autism is a disordered way of being. ASD still comes up throughout the book, particularly when referring to the diagnosis process and in medical contexts. The same goes for other ways of avoiding the word autistic: 'on the spectrum', 'differently abled', 'atypical' and so on. As a journalist, sometimes I do want a bit of vocabular variety, but I think there is power in the choices we make with language. The spectrum also tends to be misunderstood as a line from 'less autistic' to 'more autistic', rather than a kaleidoscope of different presentations and experiences, so the easiest way I can see to avoid that is to just say autistic.

The same can be said about 'high-functioning' and 'low-functioning', terms which I have avoided throughout the book, except to explain why I do not use them (on pages 73–77). Autism is an invisible and dynamic condition, and so it makes more sense to my brain to describe people as autistic in the first instance and then, if we are discussing support needs, to specify if someone has high support needs or low support needs, or maybe even support needs somewhere in between, understanding that this can also change at different stages throughout someone's life. And it is impossible to tell 'how autistic' someone is by looking at them. That is not a thing.

Neurodivergent or neurodivergence is the term for when someone's brain processes, learns and/or behaves differently from what is considered 'typical'. It comes from 'neurodiversity', a word coined by Australian autistic sociologist Judy Singer in the 1990s to name the emerging political and human rights movement by people devalued and disadvantaged by purely negative interpretations of their kind of mind. Neurodiversity can be thought of as separated into two groups – neurotypical and neurodivergent. You would not say a person is 'neurodiverse'; you would say they are 'neurodivergent', a term first used by Kassiane Asasumasu. It includes autism, but can also include ADHD, dyslexia, Tourette's and chronic mental illnesses. A community can be neurodiverse, but an individual person cannot. It is complex, and the discourse around what does and does not constitute neurodivergence is ongoing. There is no governing body, no singular consensus and no neurodivergent leader who speaks for us all.

A non-autistic person might be referred to as that, or as neurotypical if they do not identify as neurodivergent for any other reason. Neurotypical and non-autistic are not interchangeable terms, but there is crossover, and both are used throughout the book.

The conversations at times extend into wider discussions around disability. I use the term disabled person for the same reason I say autistic person. Non-disabled might be used in this context to describe someone without a disability. Some autistic people do not view themselves as having a disability, and I respect that viewpoint and choice as well. For me, I do not view the word disabled as being inherently bad, or less than, or offensive.

The disability community has taught me so much about pride and identity, and I honour them when I make that language choice for myself.

There are explainers on all the autistic terminology used throughout the book as it pops up, but for those looking for a handy guide:

Meltdown: A meltdown is an intense response to overwhelming circumstances – a complete loss of behavioural control. A meltdown is not a tantrum and is not a choice. A focus on triggers rather than behaviour helps to support an autistic person in reducing the chances of them reaching this stage of overwhelm and distress.

Shutdown: Autistic shutdowns are related to meltdowns, but are a more inward response to high stress. When an autistic person's brain becomes overloaded, they can become extremely lethargic, unable to move and unresponsive.

Stimming: Self-stimulatory behaviour, also known as stimming, is the repetition of physical movements, sounds, words or moving objects. The most recognisably autistic stims are rocking, hand-flapping and twirling, but stimming can be anything from hair-twisting to finger-tapping and flicking. Stimming is something that everybody does to some degree, but is perhaps more noticeable and done more often by autistic people. It is not the problem it is often presented as, but rather a response that might help an autistic person decrease sensory overload, adapt to a new place, or calm themselves.

I have provided a list of the research and studies mentioned throughout the text at the back of the book, a choice made for ease of reading and because this is primarily a book about people. I do not have an academic background. Like many autistic people, autism has become somewhat of a special interest to me, and I read studies like I read the news, pop culture websites and my Twitter feed. There is also a reading list for those interested in reading more widely, or deeply, about autistic people. So much of what is written about us comes from the outside in, from professionals studying us and drawing their own conclusions about what certain behaviours mean. That is unavoidable in the field of research, but I have prioritised autistic voices as best I can, and the reading list is made up entirely of work by autistic writers.

PART ONE

CURIOUS KIDS

A person who's looking at a mountain far away doesn't notice the prettiness of a dandelion in front of them. A person who's looking at a dandelion in front of them doesn't see the beauty of a mountain far away.

Naoki Higashida, *The Reason I Jump: The Inner Voice of a Thirteen-Year-Old Boy with Autism*

MICHAEL

Michael is a small boy with big feelings, whose love for Thomas the Tank Engine is growing at an exponential rate. *Did you know Thomas did not even feature in the first book on which the television series is based? It was focused on Edward, Henry and Gordon.* Michael starts his morning with Thomas, he plays with Thomas toys on the living room floor throughout the day, and he goes to sleep to a Thomas the Tank Engine bedtime story. The dark-haired child is the first for his parents Vanessa and Tom, so they are navigating their new roles while Michael is figuring out his own place in the world – one which he comes to find increasingly overwhelming. He loves the comfort of his bedroom, and cartoons on television that make him laugh. The Theo family is happy and settled in a comfortable brick home in Wollongong, as second-generation Australians with European roots. (Michael suspects this has a lot to do with his family's closeness, and the volume at which they talk.)

Vanessa and Tom wonder about his development in the way new parents do. Keeping an eye on the milestones, they assume him to be a late talker. He blows them away with what he is capable of, completing 1000-piece puzzles from the age of two. Sometimes his behaviour bewilders them, like the time he follows his mum around the grocery store taking bites out of all the fruit and vegetables he likes. A delightful sensory experience, perhaps. Or maybe just a kid being a kid. As their first child, he is their blueprint, and they quickly become experts on all things Michael. It is his kindy teacher who first points out that he might have Asperger's, which was considered a separate diagnosis to autism until 2013, when autism spectrum disorder (ASD) became the umbrella term in the *Diagnostic and Statistical Manual of Mental Disorders, Fifth Edition* (*DSM-5*). Vanessa guides him through the medical hoops, new to the language and the assessment process. Specialists confirm the kindy teacher's view with an Asperger's diagnosis, and Vanessa recalls being told Michael will never tell her he loves her or have any empathy for other people, a common belief at the time. A tragic picture of deficit and loss is painted for her in that specialist's office, but it is not one she accepts or takes on board.

•

To know Michael now, with his heart-on-his sleeve approach to life, it is hard to imagine a time when he was considered lacking in empathy. Empathy is a tricky subject in the autism world, and one I would love to unpack. It is shocking to imagine being met with that response to a child's diagnosis, but then I think back to my own child's assessments about twenty years after Michael's. Knowing that I am autistic myself, the specialists were positive and supportive, but they spent a lot of time apologising for the language needed in their reports to confirm she was autistic as well. I also vividly recall being told: 'This is the room where parents cry.' Has the medical framework changed that much? Not all autistic children will be able to say 'I love you' out loud, or be able to speak at all, but that does not mean they won't love, or learn other ways of communication.

While we are here, let's talk about empathy. First, there are two types of empathy – cognitive empathy and affective (emotional) empathy. Cognitive empathy is to do with being able to predict or pick up on what other people are feeling. Affective empathy is to feel what others are feeling. Early research and writing on autism described autistic children as being unaffected by the people around them, and without empathy. The *DSM* still hints at this, when it says, under 'social deficits', that autistic people will have 'reduced sharing of interests, emotions, or affect'. This feels as though it is specifically about cognitive empathy. It also is in direct contrast to the lived experience of me and the autistic people I know in terms of affective empathy. Michael puts it well when he describes how he has always been able to pick up on the emotions of other people, particularly his family. If his mum is stressed, he is stressed. He might not understand why, especially when a small child, but the feelings envelop him as though they are his own.

It is part of why life can feel overwhelming, but it is also part of why Michael is proud of his differences. Empathy levels will naturally vary for autistic people, just as they do for non-autistic people. Where autistic people may struggle is in detecting emotions from another person's body language or tone of voice.

Dr Damian Milton, an autistic researcher and father, proposes a different interpretation of the views around autism and empathy. He calls it the 'double empathy problem'. In simple terms, Dr Milton's theory argues that empathy is a two-way street. Autistic people and non-autistic people experience the world and express themselves differently, and therefore can both lack insight into the culture and communication styles of the other. Autistic people are often considered unable to pick up on subtext in social situations, but that subtext is constructed by non-autistic people, rather than being a universal experience. So because the non-autistic way of communicating and empathising is considered the expected way, it is treated as 'normal' and 'right', and the autistic way is considered inferior or problematic. Autistic people are labelled as having the deficit. The double empathy problem reframes this issue as being one that requires learning and compassion from both communities. Neither is the 'right' way of empathising, and non-autistic people need to learn how best to communicate with autistic people as much as the other way around.

•

Michael starts speech therapy shortly after diagnosis, which his parents hope will help him with language and self-expression.

They are adamant about imposing no limitations on Michael, insisting that he be free to follow his dreams. Every week, Vanessa takes him to see a therapist whose office is full of games, stories and charts. Speech therapy is about so much more than words and sounds, and Michael's confidence in all aspects of his communication grows.

With the addition of his younger brother Adam and sister Olivia, the family is busy, and Michael brings a lot of light and laughter into the home. He continues to find comfort in watching Thomas, as well as imitating voices from his favourite cartoons with incredible accuracy. (I am a particular fan of his Loony Tunes impressions, which he has picked up from many hours of watching the classic cartoon on VHS with his dad.) He is happy and he is loved.

As is the case for all kids, and for autistic kids in particular, the transition to primary school marks a new challenge. It is not one Michael likes to talk about.

'I was reserved, I didn't really socialise with the other students very much. I often sat alone,' he recalls.

Being away from his mum is hard for Michael, as she understands him so well. Separation anxiety was also a huge part of my early education experience, and my daughter's as well. Autistic advocate and educator Kristy Forbes describes being a parent to an autistic child as comparable to taking on the role of translator. Parents understand their child's needs, their communication style and how they react to stress and overwhelm. A teacher in a busy classroom might see a meltdown, when sensory or information overload leads to an autistic person becoming distressed and unable to cope, but they might not notice when a child shuts down, internalising their distress and withdrawing. Operating at that level of stress and overwhelm is not the ideal situation in which to learn, and this is another aspect of school Michael finds difficult. The itchy uniform and classroom noise level do not help.

Recognising his daily struggles, his mum starts a tradition – a small gesture that has rippled from his time as a primary school student and through his life to this day.

'One of my fondest memories as a kid is that my mother used to get me these chocolate treats called Yowies. She would leave them on my pillow to find when I got home from school every week. That was one of the things that led to me developing a lifelong passion for animals.'

Yowies are a chocolate that originated in Australia in 1995. Named after a legendary creature that has roots in Aboriginal oral history, each chocolate treat contains a plastic model of a native Australian or New Zealand animal, as well as a fact sheet.

As the years pass, Michael starts to find his feet. School is never his favourite place to be, but he is resilient, thanks to a strong foundation at home. Family life is the joy that breaks up the monotony of school. The Theo family prioritises time together, especially around the dinner table and on weekends. Michael has a close relationship with his father Tom, a 'deeply spiritual man', who Michael says instilled him with his old-school values.

'He took us to lots of places when we were kids; it was import-ant to him to show us the world around us,' Michael says.

He also recalls the two of them driving around Wollongong at night, particularly around the CBD and Flagstaff Hill, where there is a lighthouse and two beaches.

'I don't remember why it was just me and my dad, but it was and I really liked it.'

His parents encourage him to pursue his interests, including his fascination with modes of transport.

Autistic people often have intense passions, which can be called 'special interests'. Research shows that spending time delving into these pursuits is good for wellbeing and learning. It is strange to have this kind of joy pathologised. As autistic writer Clem Bastow says in their memoir *Late Bloomer*: 'A deficit model of autism frames special interest as something unsettling and obsessive. Why, countless parenting blogs ask, does my son sit for hours reading about the Tube? Why is my daughter constantly telling me about the mating habits of the green sea turtle?'

When he is eight years old, Michael's love of steam trains is celebrated with a daytrip to the Zig Zag Railway. *The Zig Zag Railway was first opened in the 1860s as part of the Western Railway line that linked Sydney with western New South Wales.* On a crisp autumn morning, Michael is up early, excited about the day ahead. His uncle is taking him and his cousin on the historic train ride. They queue, and Michael grows impatient as they wait for the train to arrive. The excitement fills his body, and he can't quite comprehend that his dreams are coming true today. When they finally find themselves seated on board the vintage carriage, windows open to let cool mountain air rush in, it is like ten Christmases to Michael. Steam pours from the chimney and they are on their way. For many passengers, the train is a means of visiting other tourist spots, but for Michael it is the ride itself that is the main attraction. The line crosses the Blue Mountains, rushing through dark tunnels and wrapping around steep ridges. He turns around on the leather bench seat, watching the landscape zoom by on both sides, sometimes rocking as they hug a curve. He gets a thrill when they go through a tunnel and the carriage falls into stark darkness.

The intensity and beauty of autistic joy is often overlooked in the dialogue around diagnosis and support. No doctor ever told me: 'Sometimes your child will be so happy her squeals will pour out of her like golden light. Her body will not be able to contain the energy and will move in motions of the purest freedom you have ever witnessed. She will draw more happiness from feathers than you would have thought was possible from anything. She will learn more about what she likes than you could ever dream of knowing, and you will find yourself loving those things, be they dragons or fairies or Pokémon or crystals, with more enthusiasm than you thought your mind contained.' No doctor ever told me this, but I wish they had.

●

Michael shares all of this with me over Zoom one rainy afternoon. Now 28 years old, he is quite busy these days. He was on the talk show *Ellen* a few days before our scheduled interview, as a breakout star from ABC TV's *Love on the Spectrum*. He also hosts a popular podcast called *Mr A+* (a nickname from his mum), on which he interviews media personalities, celebrities, and family and friends. I am nervous about talking to a person from the TV, so my heart clenches a little when I notice Michael yawning and looking around throughout our chat. There is a small voice in the back of my mind telling me that is supposed to be considered rude, like he is indicating his lack of interest in what I have to say. But it occurs to me that the voice telling me that it is rude is actually the rude one, because that is my neuro-typical training kicking in. Not having learned I am autistic until my twenties, I had many years in which to internalise messaging around what is the 'right' way to be. And Michael isn't being rude. He is entirely engaged, funny, clever and insightful. So why is it rude to be direct or to let our body do what it needs to do? There is no ill intent. Who got to decide that some people's natural way of being is an affront to polite society? Non-autistic people, that is who.

What I am talking about – the forcing of eye contact, or sitting still when my body needs to move – is called masking. This is when autistic people, whether consciously or not, hide or minimise their autistic traits to fit into the world. This definition feels insufficient, because it often gives non-autistic people the idea that autistic people can simply 'stop masking', like it is a literal mask that can be taken off, or maybe even like there has been a choice to deceive. Some autistic people are more successful at masking than others, whether through behavioural training or their own backgrounds and life experiences, but it always comes at a cost. Autistic professionals (by this I mean specialists in the field of autism who are also autistic) have given some wonderful insight into the mechanics and impacts of masking, which I will share a little later.

So, when I override my training, I am thrilled about the yawning. I would probably stifle my own yawns in an interview, and try to hold eye contact (or the illusion of it that comes from looking at someone's nose, or between their eyes), and I hate that I would. I love that Michael is free enough to be wholly himself on camera and in his life. That is what audiences love about him on the TV show and his podcast, and I aspire to allow myself the same freedom. I aspire to be a little more like Michael from this interview on.

JESS

Jess is a creative kid with wild, tangled hair whose body does not stop moving. A backyard trampoline provides the motion and feedback her small form craves, and Jess's parents feed her curious mind with books. So many books. Her mind likes to be in motion as much as her body does. A morning spent playing outdoors is often followed by an afternoon with a stack of books, her mum reading to her as often as she can. Jess picks up reading herself before starting school by memorising her favourite picture book, one her mum reads to her countless times, and figuring out the words and sounds from there. Early reading beyond the 'expected ability' is called hyperlexia, and it's a trait often seen in autistic people. To Jess's parents, she is bright and bookish – there is nothing to pathologise there.

As a young girl, Jess also spends a lot of time poking around the back of the garden looking for butterflies and fairies, obsessed with things with wings. She comes alive in her garden, which is small and square and a little wild as well. Perhaps this comes from the pages of the Enid Blyton novels she loves so much, or perhaps it is the first inkling of her love for animals, one which will grow throughout her life. She only wishes she had a playroom at the end of her garden, like Mollie and Peter in the *Wishing-Chair* books. And a pixie friend would be nice, too.

Jess is the oldest of three girls, born and raised in Melbourne's inner suburbs. Her parents are quiet, churchgoing and dedicated. Life follows a steady rhythm, and it suits Jess in that way. The family enjoys visiting grandparents in Tasmania. The first thing the girls always want to do when they arrive is get down onto the beach. Tasmanian beaches are rugged and windy, and feel like little pockets of paradise created just for them. A shortcut through a neighbour's yard leads directly to the sand – the perfect place for unstructured play. They run all the way there and climb and build sandcastles and swim as the adults watch on, no doubt enjoying watching them almost as much as the children enjoy playing. Jess doesn't like when the seaweed touches her legs (who does?), but this is a time of unselfconscious freedom. It is a time for her imagination, as well as her body, to stretch its legs. She collects shells and thinks about mermaids who might be hiding just below the surface, or in caves in the cliffs nearby. They all sleep well in Tasmania, because the beach has a way of tiring out the body and mind in the best possible way, like no other place can. And time with Nan and Pop is special for everyone.

Indoors, that energy does not always have an outlet, and in her bedroom sometimes Jess feels like she has so much nervous energy in her body that she needs to lie on the floor and shake her arms and legs, rolling around to get the electricity out. She tosses and turns and flails, comfortable at least in knowing she is alone in her own space for this. Still, even without anyone to bear witness to her energetic displays, Jess is aware that it is not what would be considered 'normal'.

'I would lie there and think I was crazy, like, "normal people don't do this",' she says now. 'I was also aware of parents potentially walking in, and some part of me knew I had to keep what I was doing a secret, so there was a shame element to it as well.'

Jess and I talk about how early this self-understanding of being different starts, whether it is with activity and movement (Jess also has ADHD) or in noticing how at ease others are socially (conversations feel like they require enormous effort for me). We share frustration at the stigmatisation around 'labels', because even before acquiring the ones that say 'autism', 'ADHD', 'anxiety' or 'depression', we cover ourselves with labels made of our own words and, later, harsher words applied by others.

Starting school is a huge transition, and one that has both happy and awful elements for Jess. On the first day of prep, all the new students sit on the mat while the teacher reads to the class, casually skipping over a word or two, as one does. A small hand shoots into the air. It is Jess, eager to inform her about those missing words. A confused phone call home confirms that yes, this young child has taught herself how to read, and there are ongoing discussions about whether it might be worth her skipping a grade. This is eventually nixed because Jess is, as she notes later, lacking in other areas.

There is a strong emphasis on neat handwriting – the Spalding Method – and Jess soon finds herself having extra-support lessons to help with holding a pencil properly. This provides a break from the noisy classroom, which is helpful, but Jess just wants to be able to do the thing. It does not help that Jess needs glasses and this is not picked up on until the end of the year. She is easily frustrated when she does not get the results she wants, and her energy comes out in ways she can't always seem to control.

'I remember being jealous of another girl whose work was praised for being neat. I scribbled in her book with my pencil. I had to go to the principal, who erased my scribbles and put a sticker on it. Whenever I envied another student for being neater and quieter and liked more by the teacher, I would want to lash out at them in some way.'

Jess doesn't have the language for it as a child, but says now it is likely these reactions are to do with rejection sensitive dysphoria (RSD), a common but under-researched experience for neurodivergent people, related to emotional dysregulation. It is an intense emotional response to real or perceived rejection. Like so many aspects of how I understand my autistic self, I have learned more about this from other autistic and neurodivergent people than from the diagnostic process. The most engaging writing I have found on RSD is from NeuroClastic, an online autistic collective. Author April says:

RSD can be incredibly intense, and we can feel it to the core of our being as intense physical pain, discomfort, and sensory overwhelm. It can be almost impossible to rein in these sensations when an intense episode is triggered. For me, it's chest pain ache and discomfort, and tightness, and not being able to breathe, like a knife has been stuck into my chest. It can come on so rapidly, it can consume me before I can even consciously articulate it.

School has its highs and lows like that. Jess is rewarded for her academic achievements, while simultaneously disciplined for her natural way of being. On a good day, she is rewarded more than disciplined, but there are many hard days.

When Jess is seven years old, her father gets a job that sees the whole family relocate to Tokyo, Japan. It means packing up the family home, their lives, into dozens of tea chests, clearing out old toys, saying goodbye to the routine and rhythm of everything Jess has known up until this point. Their tight family unit makes the move a little easier, although Jess struggles more than the rest. Moving overseas is tricky, with a whole new culture and new set of social rules to learn, as well as another language. Their apartment is smaller than their house in Melbourne, because real estate in Tokyo is a whole different story. Desperate to return to Australia, Jess has huge meltdowns in the first few months in Japan. Still, it does not take long for the new city to become a home. A layer of family chaos is good for that.

Jess and her sisters attend an all-girls English-language school, and in these new surrounds Jess encounters the same struggles again. While doing her work at her desk, Jess likes to rock back on her chair, feeding her body the movement it requires, and her teacher does not like this. It takes a lot of concentration to sit still – concentration that could otherwise be used on learning. The classrooms are ordered and quiet, and she feels as though she is the squeaky wheel. At the suggestion of her teacher, who thinks Jess may have ADHD, her parents, with the help of a doctor, try Jess on Ritalin®. Knowing how bright she is, her parents are sure there must be a way to help her best apply those smarts. Medication has since become a positive tool for Jess in managing her ADHD, but her first experience with it was far from ideal.

'The dosage was too high and I turned into a zombie child, which was creepy, I think. I would just sit there and stare. I had excessive focus; it was too much. We didn't try it again until we got back to Australia.'

It takes time, but Jess finds herself starting to settle in. There is order to their life in Tokyo and it has a gentle flow. She has places she likes to eat (mainly McDonald's), starts to pick up the language, and takes up rollerblading, a popular activity in Japan at the time and something that can be done around the streets because the footpaths are so well maintained. Rollerblading offers her body a fun outlet for her sensory-seeking. Autistic people have sensory experiences that differ to those of non-autistic people, and can be hypersensitive (very sensitive) or hyposensitive (experience fewer sensations) or both. Jess describes herself as feeling free when flying down the street, the wind in her hair, which is something she does not often get to feel. She also has a level of independence in Tokyo, which is confidence-building. Jess walks to and from school by herself, and sometimes stops at the shop along the way.

'I could have a polite conversation with a shopkeeper in Japanese – not fluent, but I was comfortable.'

While the time in Japan is a life-changing experience, Jess dreams of returning to Australia. She still thinks about her bedroom (pink and white, with Laura Ashley wallpaper as a border), her garden, the beach in Tasmania and her favourite parks. But idealising life in Australia makes it hard when the family does eventually return three years later.

'I built it up in my head as "everything will be better when we get back", forgetting that people who were my friends would have moved on and made other friends, and things change.'

Jess slots back into the same school, with the same classmates, but they have indeed moved on. It is jarring to be among familiar people in a familiar environment, but to no longer understand the accepted social rules. It does not help that, with the difference in school year calendars, Jess has missed half of year four because of different school calendars, but rejoining her former cohort seems the better option at the time than putting her back a grade.

Jess's ADHD diagnosis comes first and is a testament to her mother's drive to make sure she has access to all the support she needs. Jess says even she pushed back against the idea of being anything other than 'normal'. Her autism diagnosis follows a year or so later. (Research suggests 30–80 per cent of autistic children also meet the criteria for ADHD. This is an infuriatingly broad percentage range, and only looks at children, as does most research around autism.)

Her mum says it was a long road, and one that saw her come up against a lot of prejudiced and ill-informed educators, medical professionals, and bystanders. One psychiatrist even tells her she herself is seeking attention through her child because she must be depressed. The eventual diagnosis comes with a certain degree of additional understanding, but not enough to ensure that Jess's support needs are accommodated in class. Her needs are still treated as 'bad behaviours'. Then, on top of this hard transition back to Australia, plus a new diagnosis, an already difficult time is compounded by a traumatic experience with Jess's school headmistress in years five and six.

The school leader takes it upon herself to 'discipline' Jess, inaccurately and dangerously believing that this is the way to treat a neurodivergent child who is already vulnerable. The principal runs a maths support program that Jess is put in, having missed half a year of school and already struggling with maths as a subject. She also suggests to Jess's mother that Jess stay behind in her office after school to complete her homework, as she is having trouble finishing it at home. The headmistress uses these sessions to verbally abuse and berate Jess every single day for nearly two years. This is confusing to Jess, because she remembers the woman as being kind in the time before Jess moved to Japan.

'She presented one face to parents, and to the public, and then in private she was a monster. It was terrifying. She was very controlling and did not like it when children spoke out of turn.'

Even with an ADHD diagnosis the treatment continues, with the teacher labelling the diagnosis 'an excuse for poorly parented children'. Jess internalises it all. She is screamed at for her handwriting, for her colouring in, and for the way she writes out her maths problems.

'At this point, I had been in trouble so much at school I just thought that I was the problem. I thought my parents would take her side. I just never mentioned it. I didn't want to get in more trouble.'

Jess, meanwhile, suffering from post-traumatic disorder, develops trichotillomania, or hair-pulling, and dermatillomania, skin-picking, manifestations that speak to the level of stress and pressure she is under.

The ordeal doesn't end until another teacher, who knows Jess's family, overhears the headmistress screaming at Jess after school. The teacher calls Jess's mum in tears and describes how Jess is being treated. Her mother is horrified.

'When my parents got that phone call, there were no more after-school sessions. They realised the magnitude of it all. I don't think my mum has ever stopped feeling guilty about it. She was trying so hard to find people who could help and support me.'

Jess's parents offer to move her to a different school, but Jess is determined to stay, given that she is so close to graduating primary school. Besides, getting to the other suggested school seems too hard, with many steep hills and a tram ride involved.

Moving on to high school, Jess notices that her peers seem to be maturing at a much faster pace than her.

'I had a doll I would take everywhere with me. I couldn't take it to school because I wasn't allowed, but when my friends in year seven would come around to my house they were like, "You're still carrying that thing?" and I felt like I had to hide it after that.'

The girls in her year start to become more interested in boys and make-up and going to school discos. Jess knows she is supposed to feel the same, and she tries to go along with it, but something inside rebels against it. *Dolly* magazine lays out 'the rules' for growing up, and what are probably written as light-hearted articles are taken literally and seriously, as are *Sweet Valley High* and *Baby-sitter's Club* books. These books are twenty years old by this point, so Jess is sometimes acting out 'teenage behaviour' from the 1980s and 1990s, like lying that her friend's boyfriend got her front row seats to a concert when the best ones nowadays are in the mosh pit. It is fortunate that Jess's inner world remains rich, and other books still provide a safe retreat. Jess is aware that at this age she is supposed to have a celebrity crush, so she chooses Ricky Martin after seeing him on *Hey, Hey, It's Saturday.*

'So much of what I was doing was because of the books I read, and what I thought I was supposed to be doing,' she says.

As the disconnect with her peers grows, Jess begins to find comfort and community online. In the late 1990s, the internet is still something you might visit to 'browse the web' for a school assignment, and Jess gravitates towards the computer room at school more and more. The colourful Apple computers are lined up in rows, and no one bothers you there when you are hard at work. She visits Paul Jennings' website because it is in the back of one of his books, and signs up to get an email address so she can join the fan club of Irish girl group B*Witched. She makes pen pals through the mailing list and they exchange emails for years.

*B*Witched is an Irish vocal group that released music from 1997 to 2002, including their incredible hit singles* C'est la Vie *and* Rollercoaster. *According to a list of 99 B*Witched Facts on the still* *functioning website 'Sharon's B*Witched Place', vocalist Edele does not even like rollercoasters!*

'I just loved surfing around the internet, looking at things. I would get teased for that. "You're such a nerd, you're always on the computer." Back then sitting on the internet was weird. That is probably hard to imagine now.'

NOOR

Noor is a quiet child (until she isn't) who also has a voracious appetite for magical stories by Enid Blyton. As the oldest daughter in a Malaysian family headed by a strict father, she does not see herself in the pages of these books but enjoys the escapism and adventure they offer. Noor imagines herself going on adventures in forests, flying away to magical lands, and making friends with fairies and pixies and elves. Books are safe to her in a way people are not. They offer black-and-white narratives: good triumphs over evil and everything will be okay in the end. A distracted and dreamy child, Noor does not understand her parents, herself, why she cannot do the things everyone else seems to be able to do, or why things are so hard, but she can understand stories. She also loves drawing and painting – creative arts give her a space to express herself and be free. Her ability to conjure stories and art from the glorious wells of her imagination knows no bounds.

Her early years are, by all accounts, a particularly tough time in her life. Noor recounts that time with trepidation, and her own beautiful honesty.

'As one of many children, and first-born, with a most-likely undiagnosed autistic father and mother – because, let's be honest, neurodivergence doesn't come out of nowhere; it's a familial trait – I can see how triggering I was and still am to my father. And how incomprehensible I was and maybe still am for my mother,' she says.

Noor does not recall much from her early childhood, having survived a tough upbringing with an emotionally abusive father, but imagines she was at least somewhat similar to how she is now: particular in her needs, and full of energy and life. But given the unsafe nature of the family home, it was not okay for her to be truly herself.

'I've actually dissociated a lot from my childhood, so when certain things happen now, they can bring up something in me that I didn't even know was there,' she says. 'I will also have these very visceral reactions to things.'

She knows she is an impulsive kid, one who can swing between 'revved-up' high-energy bursts that can often lead to agitation and overwhelm, and more spaced-out periods of low mood and energy. Her active mind makes sleep difficult, and the more exhausted she is the harder it gets.

At school in Malaysia, like at home, she feels outside of things.

'I remember being in kindy and I was that kid outside crying. The teacher would be getting the other kids to apologise to me, and I would not understand how we got to that point. Over and over again.'

She survives the school day by keeping her head down and doing her best not to bother anyone. Perhaps a teacher would call this self-reliance, or independence, but shutdown is more of a coping mechanism than anything else. She feels the pressure to ignore her own discomfort and to prioritise the comfort of those around her. This is a defining factor of the autistic experience. Self-reflective and wise, Noor critiques this period of her life not only through the lens of self, but also down the generational line. It is all part of the one picture. She points to the signs of her parents' own neurodivergence, including her father's rigidity, and the fact that her mother did not speak until she was three or four years old. She imagines how hard it would have been for them to be neurodivergent in the era and circumstances in which they were raised.

Noor is still in primary school when the family emigrates to Australia. It is her father's wish, and one that causes him internal conflict, Noor observes. He carries a lot of internalised racism around being an Asian man, so the move to Melbourne, the idea of seeking better opportunities in the West, is one he aspires to. But the move inevitably leads to changes in the children that their father does not approve of, further fracturing the family.

As Noor points out, this should not have come as a surprise. 'If you move your family away from the motherland, they will change. They will change in ways that you might not approve of, or agree with, but that is a natural consequence of migration,' she says.

It is also a source of shame for Noor that she struggles with her mother tongue, as she thinks and reads in English instead of Malay.

'Because I became so hyperfocused in English, it became very hard for me to learn any other languages,' she says. 'I think that's a stereotype of autistic savants, being very good at language, but that's not me. That's totally not me.'

She also finds maths difficult, going against another autism stereotype.

'I still don't find it easy. Something about maths is very challenging. Maybe there is a dyscalculia thing there, not diagnosed . . . I can recognise patterns in words, but when it comes to numbers, I just really struggle.'

Dyscalculia is a condition that affects the ability to acquire arithmetical skills. It falls under the neurodivergent umbrella, and can be a coexisting condition for autistic people. Research suggests children with dyslexia (difficulty reading) are 100 times more likely to receive a diagnosis and learning support than those with dyscalculia, despite estimates that they are equally common.

Noor's father's expectations for his children are firm, and ultimately unachievable. He expects them to become doctors or lawyers, a strict trajectory that Noor says she and her siblings all rebel against in one way or another. Her mother does her best to support her children, but she is simultaneously traumatised by and dependent on her marriage, with no income of her own.

'To me, it's sad. I would want to always be connected to my children, no matter what choices they make,' Noor says.

They are also an Asian family in a part of Melbourne that does not have many Asian families at this time. Noor says the Muslim community is mostly made up of a wave of migrants from the Middle East, and there is racism between the cultural groups, fuelled by the 'model minority' myth, in which they are pitted against one another but nobody is ever enough, because they are not the 'right kind' of Australians.

'It was really tough,' she says.

In a 2018 essay published in *Meanjin*, Yen-Rong Wong notes that the phrase 'model minority' was first used to describe Asian Americans during the ascension of the civil rights movement there in the 1960s:

There are similarities between the ways in which the model minority myth has manifested in America and Australia ... The model minority myth perpetuates stereotypes about Asian Australians: that we are all good at maths, all have tiger parents who won't take anything less than an A, so consequently, all excel academically and are forced to learn a musical instrument from an impossibly young age. We are all studying to be lawyers or doctors or dentists or some other profession that will make us a lot of money. We are all meek and submissive – especially the women – and even though there are those of us out there who are supposedly domineering and seductive, we can ultimately be tamed. We are quiet, obedient. We don't complain. We keep our heads out of trouble.

But the model minority is just that, a myth, because Asianness is not a monolith – Asia is much more than East Asia. It is a myth because these traits have been used to argue for the successful integration of migrants into Australian society. It is a myth because it is used to perpetrate the image of Australia as 'happy', 'multicultural', free of racism, and to deny the atrocities committed against Aboriginal and Torres Strait Islander peoples in the name of colonialism.

So much of Noor's story goes against the autism stereotypes we are shown in media and research. While the term 'autism' was coined in 1908 to describe schizophrenic patients, a lot of the early research around what we now understand as autism was undertaken by two doctors in the 1940s: Hans Asperger and Leo Kanner. Both studied young white boys exclusively. While work has been and is being done to dispel misconceptions around autism in relation to gender, culture and ethnicity, it is still a commonly held belief that autism presents in one particular way. This results in lower diagnosis rates in girls and trans and gender-diverse people, as well as people of colour. And that can mean less support, both financially and emotionally, as well as less under-standing and more stigma. This is a big part of why Noor has shared her story. She has participated under a pseudonym, and explains why.

'That is one thing I speak about with a friend of mine, another Muslim woman of colour, who is probably also autistic. We don't have the white privilege to be able to be out and proud and write about being autistic, because our competence will be questioned in various aspects of life, unfortunately, because of racism, ableism, all the rest of it. That has always been my life. I have always been fragmented.'

While most people recognise the word 'racism' (even if their understanding is surface level), 'ableism' can sometimes draw blank stares. Ableism is discrimination and social prejudice against people with disabilities. This includes things like stereotypes, language choices, bias, as well as more extreme examples of oppression, such as physical, mental and emotional abuse. Even among those who love and support us, many still do not view autistic people as the experts on autism. Autistic voices are often shunned in favour of doctors, parents and people in support roles.

Autistic support specialist Kristy Forbes says even she was susceptible to viewing herself as an 'autism expert', long before she knew she was autistic.

'Working in the field, being [an] early childhood, primary and secondary educator, having all this professional development about what autism is and how to teach autistic children, I then worked as a social worker, supporting educators and going into the homes of people whose children were autistic. Now if you had asked me back then if I knew much about autism, I would have said, "Yes, I am an expert, I know so much about autism." Now I look back and go, "That was all textbook stuff. There was no applied learning, no lived experience, I knew absolutely nothing." Because if it [had] helped me, and if I really did know so much about autism, I would have known I was autistic.

I would have [recognised] that my children who were diagnosed later were autistic. But no, my mind was so focused on the textbook autism, whereas now my understanding of autism is so completely different. I definitely left behind this medical disorder approach, and seeing it as separate to people. That's not something I believe anymore, or experience myself. Now, for me personally, autism is an identity and a culture. Neurodivergence is an identity and culture.'

In Melbourne, Noor starts attending a private Muslim school, and finds it thrilling to be recognised as competent in the subjects she enjoys. Stories still play a huge role, particularly as a self-regulating activity.

'Books were always encouraged. I learned to always have a book, find a corner, read it, everything will be fine,' she says.

Noor remembers certain hard moments in her childhood, including when she first thinks her parents are going to get divorced. She develops dermatillomania, and she still skin-picks as an adult.

'I realise it is very common for autistic girls and women,' she says. 'It's completely involuntary.'

Noor still loves telling her siblings stories, and while she is not super athletic, she enjoys taking part in sports. Things get better both at home and in her school community by the time her younger siblings are older.

'That is the trial of being the oldest, being the experimental child, for lack of a better word. To always be the first one to break through barriers. And there were many.'

There is a lot Noor looks back on with sadness.

'What would have helped [are] education, diagnosis – all the things I can give to myself [now] and heal the little girl inside me,' she reflects. 'That is the hope, at least; there has got to be some meaning through all of this.'

CHLOË

When Chloë's grandmother gifts her a paint-by-numbers kit for her seventh birthday, the sensitive, rule-loving girl bursts into tears. The box advises that the kit is for ages eleven and up.

'I was distraught. I was just like, "Nan, I'm turning seven, why would you give me something I'm not able to do?" I put it in a cupboard and wouldn't touch it until I was old enough,' she recalls with a smile.

The age-inappropriate gift is a blip in an otherwise joyous day, and Chloë loves the ceremony that comes with a celebration like this: the cake, the singing, the presents. Birthday parties can be relied on to follow a routine, and if they are just with family, they are not socially difficult either. Chloë's literal thinking is on display here and reminds me so much of my own. If an event starts at a certain time – say, 2 pm – I will want to get there at 2 pm.

I have learned that this is not necessarily what is expected, especially at parties held by adults, but my body is still flooded with stress at the idea of running late.

Autism is constantly mentioned in whispers around Chloë, but never directly to her. Nor is an official diagnosis sought. She attributes people's suspicions that she is autistic to her being very good at maths and science, bad at making friends, and her lack of interest in playing made-up games with her toys.

'I loved setting up scenarios . . . So I would make the furniture, make the clothes, and then my sister would want to play and I would say, "No thank you, that's boring."'

She is also heart-wrenchingly sensitive. If anyone tells her off, even mildly and for the most minor infractions, she bursts into tears. There is an instance when she is painting at the kitchen table with her sister while her dad has a meeting. He returns to find her sister and quite a fair amount of the house covered in paint, while Chloë has only let a single drop fall into a groove of the wood. Her dad tells the girls he is disappointed in them, and while her sister is unfazed, Chloë starts to bawl.

'I would just get so upset about letting people down,' she says.

•

Growing up in regional Western Australia, school is the only real option for friendships. Her first school is in the city and fairly large, but when her mum moves to the Great Southern region Chloë is enrolled in a tiny rural school. Being perceived as a 'city kid' compared to her cohort, Chloë has a hard time fitting in.

'I remember playing cops and robbers, and it got really rough, and I got really hurt, so I complained to the teacher and that game got banned. So I was not popular.'

Her intelligence is also the first and sometimes only thing the other children can see.

'We did a booklet where we wrote a compliment for everyone and every page of my book said, "You're so good at maths", "You're good at maths". I have personality and feelings too. I hated being boiled down to my brain and just being smart. I am a nice and caring person. People really go all out to compliment perceived intelligence, but there are so many other aspects to me. But at school I was *just* the smart kid.'

The stereotype that all autistic people are good at maths or science can be traced back to those early studies by Hans Asperger, whose case studies showed 'precociousness in arithmetic'. It can also be linked to certain media representations of autistic people as having savant skills, including the scene in *Rain Man* where the doctor asks Charlie Babbitt (played by Tom Cruise) about the 'special abilities' of his brother Raymond (played by Dustin Hoffman). Charlie explains that Raymond has a good memory and can 'count toothpicks in seconds'. The doctor then tests Raymond with some sums, which he nails, and Charlie is blown away. He thinks Raymond should work for NASA.

While it is the case that some autistic people are particularly skilled with numbers, or science, or in other areas, that is not the whole story, as is outlined in one research paper: 'Even if savant-ism mostly comes with autism, the majority of cases of autism do not have savantism. In movies, however, there are hardly any autistic characters not having savant skills . . . The unrealistic stereotype of autistic savants having supercomputers for brains, to mention but one example, may create the myth of autistic persons having no feelings.'

Chloë wishes to be seen by her peers as a whole human being, rather than purely for what her brain can achieve. She feels her emotions strongly. At times, especially when she is young, they can feel too strong, too much. Chloë has what she calls 'spectacular meltdowns', which seem to further disconnect her from her peers. They start as rumbles, and the warning signs are there for people who know what to look for: increased agitation, sensory overwhelm and emotional dysregulation. They climax in a lot of screaming and crying, before exhaustion sets in. And as she grows older and gains an understanding of how other people perceive these meltdowns, there is shame too.

The best description I have come across for the lead-up to autistic meltdowns (if we ignore the dehumanising aspect of the analogy) is the 'Coke bottle effect', which likens an autistic person, particularly a child, to a bottle of fizzy soft drink. Whenever something stressful happens in the day, the bottle is shaken. Stress factors might include being urged to get dressed and leave for school in a hurry, or sensory stressors like being too hot, or an itchy uniform. The bottle is shaken, shaken, shaken. Bright lights in the classroom, loud classmates, an unexpected change to the schedule. Shake, shake, shake. And on it goes throughout the day. The teacher might be observing a 'well-behaved' child, but when enough pressure has built inside the bottle, the child's lid is going to blow. Sometimes that might be when they get home, but it might occur in the classroom, or in the school playground. It is why I tense up in discussions around my child's support needs when an educator observes, 'But she is *so* well behaved in class.' I know the toll it takes on stress levels and mental health to keep everything inside the bottle, and I know how it feels to completely blow my lid.

The other side to this sensitivity is that sometimes Chloë finds ways to harness it, in the sensory sense. When she is a young, she loves doing 'dizzy whizzies', spinning herself around and around with her arms wide. 'I would do this for hours,' she says.

The euphoria and rush she feels from this is limitless, and in those moments she experiences pure joy.

TIM

Tim describes himself as 'different from day one'. The youngest of four children, two girls and two boys, Tim lives in Melbourne with his family and is doted on as the adorable youngest child. His parents met at university, both students from Hong Kong who came to Australia to study, and they raise their children with strong family values and connection to their Chinese culture.

For a while Tim thinks he has two mothers, because his oldest sister takes such good care of him. He enjoys time with his siblings, and likes to laugh. A visual thinker with huge sensory overload and information-processing issues, Tim has difficulty understanding language. The feeling of overwhelm intensifies as he grows older, especially as a toddler around the children of family friends, or at social activities for children his age, like playgroups. While other children seem to be able to respond to questions, and understand what they are being asked to do, Tim, with his struggle to decipher language, finds it a challenge. He feels overwhelmed by the expectation that he respond like other children. Laughing makes him feel more in control, though, as does humming, which helps him to manage sensory overload.

In the early years, Tim's mother Sarah tells me, she has trouble accepting that her youngest child has differences, and she tries to ignore the signs, including his lack of speech, repetitive behaviour, and proneness to distress and meltdowns. While he has some early words, Tim is non-speaking after fourteen months, and is eventually diagnosed as autistic at the age of three. The diagnosis marks a turning point for Sarah, and she begins to investigate the literature on autism that is available, and looks into the various programs on offer.

'Unfortunately, although the professionals we consulted were well-meaning and committed to helping, there was a pervasive medicalised deficit model of autism, and we were basically told that Tim would remain severely disabled and need high levels of daily support and supervision,' Sarah says.

In Sarah's reading just after Tim's diagnosis, mainly written by academics and researchers, the prevalent account centres around a deficit-based model. On the other hand, Sarah is driven by a strong desire to provide Tim with a meaningful and full life that builds on his strengths and affirms his natural way of being.

'I immersed myself in the work of autistic authors like Temple Grandin and Donna Williams, whose books helped enormously in giving me insights into the inner world of autism and how their behaviours are part and parcel of differences in neurological functioning.'

Temple Grandin is an American autistic scientist and animal behaviourist who was one of the first autistic people to document her insights about autism. She is a powerful autistic advocate and has written several books, including: *Emergence: Labeled Autistic* (1986; with Margaret M. Scariano); *Thinking in Pictures, and Other Reports from My Life with Autism* (1995); *The Autistic Brain: Thinking Across the Spectrum* (2013; with Richard Panek); and, for younger readers, *Calling All Minds: How to Think and Create Like an Inventor* (2018). Donna Williams, who died in 2017, was an Australian autistic author and teacher who wrote four memoirs, including *Nobody Nowhere: The Extraordinary Biography of an Autistic Girl* (1992). Sarah read Williams' writings on autistic differences in sensory and information processing, anxiety and other challenges, and later consulted with Donna Williams to implement aspects of Tim's home program.

With her background in psychology and education, Sarah puts her newly acquired knowledge to work in helping Tim to understand and navigate the neurotypical world. And work she does.

Tim does not develop an understanding of language until the age of five or six. His mother devises a program catering to Tim's visual strengths by reading lots of books to him, and making books with photographs about daily routines and their family life. The photo books provide Tim with the opportunity to pair words with images in a dawning understanding of language. Tim also teaches himself to translate images into words for expressive language.

It is estimated that 25 to 30 per cent of diagnosed autistic people will never develop spoken language. With support, many non-speaking autistic people will go on to learn other communication methods, such as sign language and augmentative and alternative communication (AAC).

Describing his communication journey, Tim says, 'This journey to communication is grounded in the ability to make sense of the world and to organise this information for engagement with others, hence repetitive and expressive components start from infancy.'

Tim's dad is a strong support for the family, but he works long hours, seven days a week. This means Sarah is responsible for the daily care of Tim and his three older siblings, who are aged between eight and fifteen when Tim is diagnosed. Their daily timetable is extremely full.

'I had to juggle the different demands of the children, two at high school and one at primary school, and Tim mostly at home, involved in early intervention, kinder and intensive home programs,' Sarah recalls. 'Fortunately, Tim's siblings offered help, especially my two daughters, and they played with and supervised him while I was doing housework or delving into more information on autism.' Tim's two grandmothers are also generous with their help, offering to babysit when needed.

Sarah is able to manage it all thanks to her organised routine and the fact that Tim is fairly compliant when it comes to outings like shopping or visiting family and friends.

'It was a steep learning curve when Tim became resistant and did not follow instructions,' she says. 'Many times, I had to revise my own assumptions to accommodate his sensory and other needs, such as high anxiety. I learned to be flexible very quickly.'

A quiet yet powerful advocate, Sarah tries everything the specialists recommend, including intensive speech therapy and behavioural programs, as well as doing mountains of her own research. After her initial resistance, she is determined to embrace Tim's differences.

The bond between Tim and Sarah is magnificent to witness in action. They have their own flow. Sarah says they are very in tune with one another's feelings, which can have its good moments and its tricky ones. Tim is grateful to Sarah for helping him to find a communication style that works for him.

'Mum designed programs that take into account my visual strengths and love of music and rhythm,' Tim says. 'I pretty much developed an understanding of language, people and the world through her programs.'

•

Tim starts his education at a school for autistic children, as recommended by his specialists at the time. He finds it chaotic and difficult to navigate, and it does not help his development. Sarah suggests integrating him into mainstream schooling, but the idea meets with resistance, as only students with speech are given opportunities through an integration program at the time. Sarah continues to advocate, and after Tim is badly bitten by another student, she tries something more drastic.

'I went to a country school which accepted him full-time.'

Tim spent the first term of year two there, facing challenges in adjustments to a different school away from familiar environments. Luckily, he is then able to return to Melbourne to be fully integrated at a mainstream primary school. With accommodations in place, school becomes a positive experience for Tim. It can be exhausting and taxing on his energy reserves at times, but he also embraces the experience and the learning. He loves books, especially the informational kind that offer insight into how people from different cultures, backgrounds and traditions live. He also shows a strong propensity for maths, and the supplementary home-based program Sarah has devised based on his interests and strengths is adapted to suit his emerging capabilities. Concrete aids, designed from the Montessori method, also help Tim to grasp mathematical concepts. For example, with a simple tape measure representing a number line, Tim starts to understand numbers as a tool to quantify objects. With the groundwork in place, Tim picks up more advanced mathematical concepts with ease, and once he understands something, he can apply it in more and more complex scenarios. Tim also starts reading chapter books, which increase his understanding of the world and people. As Tim's home program exceeds what he learns at school, Sarah and Tim often extend his school-based learning to dovetail with his interests.

By the age of nine, Tim is literate and numerate, but he does not have a reliable means for self-expression. He is introduced to various augmentative and alternative communication (AAC) methods, and identifies a style of type-to-talk communication known as partner-assisted typing (PAT) as his preference. This method is a huge success. PAT means that Tim is given the physical support required to type on a speech-generating device. This physical touch provides feedback of his body in space, and helps initiate arm movement towards typing. At first, Sarah and other facilitators provide Tim with physical touch on his wrist and arm, fading support to his shoulder and back when he becomes more proficient. With lots of practice over the years, Tim is becoming more independent of physical support but needs emotional and regulatory support to type smoothly.

'I took up PAT very readily but to [type] efficiently, I had to overcome my movement difficulties such as challenges in initiation, perserveration and focus,' he says. 'I worked very hard, as PAT was a game-changer.'

Once Tim learns to type to communicate, his discussions with his mum become a highlight for both of them. They sit in the kitchen and talk about everything from minor incidents of their days to broader political, social and cultural ideas. Tim has a strong sense of justice from a young age, never wanting any other student in his class to be treated unfairly, and Sarah is constantly blown away by how he sees and describes his experiences of the world. I see this for myself when Tim explains how well he can perceive the message behind other people's words, something he attributes to being attuned to people's feelings rather than what they say.

'There are so many challenges in a world that doesn't understand, acknowledge or accept diversity I won't be able to list them all. Because of these challenges, I find autistic people learn to be resilient and to navigate the world with our strengths of mind, heart and purpose,' he says.

A SIDENOTE ON FUNCTIONING LABELS

To misquote from the beloved 1990s movie *10 Things I Hate About You* . . .

Q: Autistic people can supposedly be 'high-functioning', and they can be 'low-functioning', but can anyone ever be 'medium-functioning'?

A: I think they can in Europe.

I'm joking, of course, but I truly believe it is worth considering why these labels are still being used, and who they benefit. Childhood is generally the time when these labels are applied, for those with formal identification at a young age, and they do not benefit either the person who is 'high', because it minimises their needs, nor the person who is 'low', because it strips them of their agency and humanity. And I have never heard people in the autistic community argue among themselves about who is more autistic. The call is not coming from inside the house.

Michael, Jess, Noor, Tim and Chloë have different support needs from me, from one another, and even from themselves at different stages throughout their lives. To remove functioning labels from dialogue around these people as human beings is not to deny that they have challenges; it is to affirm that they are not effigies constructed purely of how they present to the world. Their value does not come from what capital they can produce, or how much or how little support they need from other people.

Autistic advocate and educator Kristy Forbes says it makes most sense to understand that autism is a way of being, and that there are categories (perhaps these might be sensory sensitivities, processing, social challenges and speech, to name a few) into which people will fall in different places, with different strengths and challenges.

'The other thing to note is that people who are assumed to be "high-functioning" are the people in our community who fit into the stats around suicide, or attempted suicide, and who are in mental health facilities,' she says.

According to research, the rate of suicide is three times higher in autistic people than non-autistic people. It is particularly high in autistic teenagers and young adults. In several studies, this is linked to social isolation and poor access to support.

Kristy continues: 'And the people who are deemed "low-functioning", or "severely" autistic – how insulting and offensive it is to say those things about them. And then to read books written by those same people, or to communicate with them in ways other than verbal communication, and to learn that their capacity is completely undermined because we are correlating it with their sounds, the way they move their body.'

Another element to this conversation that is often skipped over is masking. Many autistic people, diagnosed or undiagnosed, are taught or teach ourselves to present in a certain way, as less autistic, so that we are safe, so that we fit in, so that we are not targeted. Kristy outlines how for so many of us it is a lose-lose situation.

'When we have early intervention, the goal is to have us mask; the goal is to make us appear as though we are doing really well even if we are not. So then people say you're "high-functioning", or "mildly autistic" – it is undermining.'

Autistic people are so much more than their behaviours, coping mechanisms and communication styles. A lot of discussions that involve these functioning labels also tend to project forward into a child's later life with anxieties about what they will or will not be able to do, to be, to achieve. As a parent to a young autistic child whose support needs are high, I do understand where that comes from, especially when a parent's first introduction to autism is through the 'autism as tragedy' lens. Parents worrying about their children's future is not something that is exclusive to parents of autistic children. But the truth is, we do not know and cannot know what kinds of lives our children are going to have when they grow up. It is out of our control. What we can do is meet their support needs now, and validate those needs by treating them as needs and not as inconveniences or bad behaviour, or as something that causes us grief. Celebrate them for who they are, for what they love, and support them in the ways they need.

Kristy Forbes highlights the importance of nurturing the parent–child relationship.

'Parents need to understand that the way we consider ourselves and the way we treat ourselves impacts the connection we have with our child. I don't know about you, but my children are like a mirror for me. Even when I don't know I am having a hard time, they will show me. It will show up in their behaviour, their anxiety, the way they connect with me. And so often we go about saying that a child is struggling with A, B or C because they are autistic. Sometimes, if we put the word autistic aside and look at the relationship at home between parent and child, a lot of our challenges and a lot of our child's challenges have to do with how we are connected.

'I work with families to encourage a natural curiosity about their children, their behaviour, their autonomy and thinking processes, but also a natural curiosity about how we respond to that, how we react to that, and what sits within us that triggers those responses and reactions. Because there are a lot of parents who may not even realise they are carrying their own trauma, their own experiences, their own stuff that sits there – unseen, unheard and unknown – that is causing us to react to our children in ways that we don't have to.'

Supporting a child with high support needs can be hard, and there is not enough support for parents in these roles. Community is vital, and connection with other parents raising autistic children can be a literal lifesaver. When I was a new parent and compared myself to others, it often left me feeling as though I was doing something wrong, I was not enough, I needed to change.

A sidenote on functioning labels

People were so quick to tell me how my child would be and should be, and most of them were wrong, because they did not understand or even consider that an autistic child's needs might be more, and might be different. The comparison game is terrible for self-esteem, and breaking free of it all is the first step in raising an autistic child in an affirming way.

FROM WHERE THEY STAND: YOUNG AUTISTIC PERSPECTIVES

I asked some autistic children and young adults to share their interests and thoughts on love and autism, because the more autistic voices in this conversation, the better. And in my experience, young people are the ones who really know what's up.

•

Eleven-year-old Emmett from Ballarat loves *Minecraft*, his mum and his soft toys. He describes being autistic in such a perfect way: 'My brain works differently and sometimes it feels like I've eaten too much Skittles.' He doesn't like a lot of the challenges of being autistic, but loves his big imagination and wants people to know: 'I'm just a normal guy.'

Nine-year-old Emmie from the Sunshine Coast loves her family and her two dogs, Peppa and Kransky, 'because they are amazing'. She says: 'Love is when I care.' Emmie knows that being autistic means she is special, and says the hardest part is 'when I am tired or have to wear clothes'. 'I wish that people knew I was autistic when my clothes or togs aren't done up right.'

Felix, who is twelve and from Melbourne, says love is feeling warm and happy and content, 'because someone or an animal makes you feel like you belong'. Felix loves his dog and family. He describes autism as a spectrum where 'people feel different or act different or their senses are different to other people's in varying ways'. The best bit is thinking differently from most people and the hardest part is when people don't understand and reject him. He says: 'I wish more people knew about autism and understood it's how some people are. If more people knew, then less people would be rejected because people wouldn't think they were weird.'

Eleven-year-old Flynn, from the Sunshine Coast, loves cats (and any animals for that matter), as well as his parents and *Minecraft*. For him, autism means 'you can do things other people can't but you find difficult things other people can do easily'.

'I can do a lot of things other people can't do, like designing worlds in *Minecraft*,' he says, but things like handwriting can be difficult.

He wishes people knew that certain things can be hard for autistic people and to help those who are struggling.

Sixteen-year-old Jordan, from Adelaide, loves Lego, Batman, DC Comics and Disney. He describes love as being about caring. He describes autism as 'people thinking differently, being a little bouncy and unstable at times'. He notes that this is 'in my point of view, as I'm bouncy'.

The best thing about being autistic is 'being able to view things differently from everyone else', and some hard parts are low muscle tone and people 'not understanding where we are coming from'.

'I wish that people knew that autism can affect speed, understanding and strength. We didn't ask to be this way, it is how the world works. It is more than point of view, much more. It doesn't matter how much autism someone has, they can still have similar traits to someone with level 3 autism,' he says.

Seven-year-old Aggie from the Sunshine Coast says there are different kinds of love, like romantic love, friend love, family love and love for things.

She really loves her soft toys, including Shorty the sausage dog.

'I also love my mum, who is writing this book, Dad and all my family,' she says.

Aggie says autism is like when someone is different from

another person, but there are lots of people in the world who have autism, like her, Shorty, her mum and her cousin Emmie.

'The best part of being autistic is my mum is really understanding when I'm sad. And having a sensory swing. The hardest bits are crying when things are hard,' she says. 'I wish more people knew that autistic people can get overwhelmed a lot and you should treat them kindly.'

Thirteen-year-old Amelia from Melbourne, who is non-speaking and an emerging writer, wrote some beautiful responses to my questions.

Love knows no conditions. It shows no limits. Many people spend many years looking for unconditional love, but enter a love with many restrictions. The key to love is made with three ingredients. The first is vulnerability. To have love, you need to be open to its many forms. Just like when you are learning to ride a bike, you need to be open to the idea that someone will let go.

Second is giving over your expectations and creating new memories. So many people hold on to memories of pain and hurt that they forget to enjoy their progress. Life offers so much more than you remember.

Last is acceptance. Imagine how much you could give, or you could see how worthy you are. Remind yourself just how incredible you are. Treat yourself the way you treat the ones you love.

When asked who and what she loves, Amelia wrote:

I love so many things. I love wholly and abundantly. My love has many ranges; I love people, things, food and songs. I love my family; my dear mom, beloved dad, older brothers Geordie and Noah and my best friend/sister Kalliope. I love my communication partner/soul sister Sarah, my past carers and current ones.

I also love movies and music, I find myself so empowered by audio and visual creativity. My favourite singers are Noah Kahan [and] Lorde, and Sarah has a most amazing voice too. I love to taste new flavours, and to enjoy familiar ones as well.

But above all, I love to dance. It is how I connect to the Mother Earth and how I connect to myself.

•

These responses make me emotional, when I think about the next generation of autistic people and the level of self-understanding and pride they are growing up with, when I think about how they will, and how they already are, advocating for one another, and because I feel so lucky and grateful to learn from them.

PART TWO

GROWING PAINS

I believe we could paint a better world if we learned to see it from all perspectives, as many perspectives as we possibly could. Because diversity is strength. Difference is a teacher. Fear difference, you learn nothing.

Hannah Gadsby, autistic comedian

CHLOË

Chloë starts dating her first boyfriend when she is eleven and he is twelve. The star-crossed tweens first meet at the park near their small country school; Chloë is the new kid in the town he has grown up in, and the only girl remotely close to his age. He rides his bike a lot with his friends, and plays a lot of PlayStation. Chloë thinks he is cute and nice. It feels as much like love as any eleven- and twelve-year-old can feel and comprehend. They spend time together when they can and tell each other 'I love you'. After three months, which is quite a long time at this age, Chloë is unceremoniously dumped. The culprit: playground politics.

'His friends hated me – that was that,' she says.

Brutal. And so begins her adolescence.

Chloë's friendships in high school all seem to be with outcast people of one variety or another. It is something she is aware of on some level, and grows to hate. She wants 'normal' friends. She wants the picture-perfect girl gang friendship group, and the quintessential best friend forever. That is what the movies tell her she should have, and that is what she wants.

'It's funny, because I used to really pull away [from the outcast kids]; at a subconscious level I knew there was a reflection there. Obviously, I must be part of this group. It's frustrating because had I known [I was neurodivergent] it would have been much easier,' she says.

Teachers who pick up on the social difficulties Chloë is facing, but who lack the skills or the education to identify what is going on, tell her she will find her people at university.

'Primary school teachers are taught to look out for [students who might be autistic], but not high school teachers. Because I went to a country school, these teachers taught me for five or six years. They really did know me. So it endlessly frustrates me that it was never addressed. People knew, but because I was smart and not causing any issues, it didn't go any further.'

The whisperings around the 'A' word continue. And so does the bullying. Chloë finds her directness and sensitivity put her at odds with a lot of her classmates. While the rest of the students go outside at lunchtime to run around and let off some steam on the school oval, Chloë hangs out with her teachers, sometimes just for a chat and sometimes to help them mark tests.

'People didn't get along with me very well, or I didn't get along with others very well. I'm not sure which it was,' she says. 'It's hard because, being in the country, school is the only option for friendships.'

She is put up a grade for maths class, and the kids in the higher grade hate that she is younger than them but doing better.

'I remember once one kid got a higher score than me and really wanted to rub it in my face that he beat me. I was like: good job,' she says.

'That year group – ugh. My teachers wanted me to skip a year, but I remember not wanting to be around those particular people. I remember feeling like, please do not let me skip, because they would despise me even more if I was in all their classes.'

At home, Chloë can now recognise that her whole family is neurodivergent; nothing seems out of place, as it is their normal.

'It is interesting because, on one hand, why wasn't it picked up then? But on the other hand, when your whole family is like that, why would it be picked up?'

Chloë says that she used to think she wasn't particularly literal, but looking back there are some instances that suggest otherwise. One such time is when, as a teenager, she is at her dad's place and his girlfriend at the time has two young kids. Chloë is tasked with keeping an eye on them while her dad and his partner duck into town to pick up a couple of things. Her dad says, 'Don't let them out of your sight,' because they live on a hobby farm with endless ways for a small person to injure themselves, and also, 'Don't let them in the house,' because the house is not child-proof, and there are too many ways they could get into trouble there too. Basically, her dad wants her to play with the kids on the porch and in the garden. But once she is left on her own, Chloë finds that she really needs a drink of water, and panics given the parameters of her babysitting gig. She can't go inside and leave the younger kids unattended, but she can't take them into the house with her. Nor can she use the hose, as that water is not supposed to be for drinking. Chloë is nothing if not ingenious, though; she manages to fashion a harness for the kids, and ties them to the front porch.

'I watched them the entire time, literally did not take my eyes off them, and ran into the kitchen to get a drink of water,' she recalls.

This happens to be the exact moment at which her dad and his girlfriend arrive home, and they are surprised and more than a little upset about the scene they encounter.

'They were like, "Why didn't you just take them into the house while you got a drink?", and I remember thinking, "You told me I couldn't, this is very obvious, I don't know what you're missing."'

I too can draw on so many examples of when things have got lost in translation like this, between the autistic directness and taking people at face value, and the non-autistic assumption that people will read between the lines and understand what has been implied without further explanation. One of the hardest learning curves for me was on play dates and hangouts with friends. If I was invited over to a friend's house and they didn't mention anyone else was going to be there, I would assume I was going there for some quality one-on-one time. I remember the anxiety and panic of arriving at a friend's house to find her already hanging with somebody else. I hid in a room to try to calm down, and her mother admonished me for acting 'selfish and spoiled'. It was rough. I now text friends before most events to ask who will be there – or, even better, have friends who understand they should let me know.

●

As a teenager, there is a time when Chloë has a core group of friends at school, her absolute dream, and they hang out together at their own special table before the bell goes. She feels as though she is the quirky best friend character in the teen movie of her life. It does not last long. One of the other girls tells her she must leave the group, and that they are no longer friends.

'I was devastated,' Chloë says.

She is still as emotionally sensitive as she was when she was a kid, to the point where a teacher telling her off sends her into a flood of tears.

'The teacher didn't know what to do, so he sent me out of the classroom. Another teacher walked past and asked why I was out of class. I remember replying, bawling, "I'm not kicked out – I just needed a minute."'

She starts using Tumblr, a microblogging and social networking website, and makes a lot of friends there. The internet is a scarce resource at school, but Chloë gets permission to use it for homework.

'Tumblr wasn't banned in schools until I was in year twelve – the Department of Education banned it – and I made a lot of online friends there. I had a lot of friends all over the place. I think online friendships were what got me through. I spent hours and hours talking to people [online].'

Tumblr feeds Chloë's love for Australian pop-punk trio Short Stack. Her devotion is unwavering from when she is in year seven until they break up, when Chloë is in year twelve. She commits in the way autistic people are so good at doing.

'I was friends with one of the roadies' siblings on Facebook; it went deep,' she laughs.

'Autistic people are great at being fangirls. Any time someone would [mention] Short Stack, everyone would look at me . . .'

At school, Chloë gravitates to the older kids, but when she gets to year twelve they have all gone. Something changes in her approach to friendships. She stops caring what other people think and starts having fun by herself.

'I remember sitting in the year twelve common room, all the couches were full except the couch I was on, and someone comes into the room, looks around and squishes onto another couch instead of sitting next to me. Well, damn the lot of you! I put my legs up [on the couch and stretched out]. I stopped caring. That was a really big change, and that was needed,' she says.

There are several studies about autism and bullying that show autistic young people are more likely to be bullied than their non-autistic classmates. According to Australian research, autism is the 'top risk factor' for bullying among neurodevelopment conditions, including ADHD, Tourette syndrome, learning disabilities, intellectual disabilities and epilepsy. The same study shows autistic students are more likely to be bullied in high school than primary school. The authors of the study have suggested that neurodiversity and inclusiveness should be integrated into school-based anti-bullying programs, including teaching kids that neurodiversity is a difference rather than an impairment, encouraging kids to use proper language, learning about how autistic people might react to stress differently and running bullying-prevention workshops at high schools, because of the higher risk of bullying for autistic students at this age.

Chloë reflects on this time of her life as being particularly difficult, and wonders whether autistic and neurodivergent friendships are just fundamentally different.

'I've had different phases of friends, but I never have friends for a long time. I don't know if that is me getting bored, or them getting bored of me,' she says. 'I'll have different phases of intensity of friendships, and I like that about neurodivergent friendships. We don't need constant check-ins to know we're still friends. We could go months, and then hang out. And it's great.'

Neurotypical expectations are still on the periphery, but Chloë says she has a deeper understanding about how friendships work for her.

'I still dream of having the bestie, the neurotypical bestie who is the one you go to with everything. But I really am starting to realise that I have friends for different things and that's okay,' she says. 'Those kinds of friendships aren't really modelled, though. All I saw was the right way to have friends is to have a core group of friends, and I always felt really off not having that.'

JESS

Sitting in a counsellor's waiting room with her mum, twelve-year-old Jess starts to pull pamphlets from the rack on the wall to pass the time, picking them at random. It is the only entertainment; the magazines are years out of date and all the crosswords have been done. Inside these brochures is information about grief, and depression, and addiction. The text is always accompanied by stock images of people walking on beaches or sitting on nondescript couches with their heads in their hands. When Jess picks up the pamphlet about Asperger's, she is surprised to find almost the entirety of her life struggles neatly summarised in five or six dot points.

'I showed it to Mum and said, "This might be me."'

Her mum is supportive, but Asperger's has only been added as a separate diagnosis in the *DSM-4* a couple of years prior, which makes finding someone to diagnose it a challenge. It is not the counsellor they see today. The autism specialist who is eventually able to give Jess a diagnosis the following year is used to seeing people with higher support needs and speaks to thirteen-year-old Jess as though she is in preschool. This goes down like a lead balloon, and Jess stonewalls her.

'She [wrote] in her notes that I had a strange way of talking, but I was trying to use the most bored voice possible because I did not want to cooperate,' Jess says. 'I was really sarcastic. I hated people treating me differently.'

●

After the trauma of her late primary school experience, Jess finds the stress of the transition to high school completely overwhelming, and a new diagnosis is too much to process. By this stage, her mum has taken her to countless specialists, including speech therapists, occupational therapists and several different psychologists in search of the support Jess needs to understand how to work *with* her way of being rather than against it. Jess, meanwhile, has grown increasingly angry, frustrated and distrustful of the whole process.

The overwhelm is intense. It seems as though everyone else is living their life on fast forward, and Jess is watching them all pass by in a blur. Video games like *Super Mario*, which she plays on her Nintendo 64, keep her tethered to her own life. She passes the hours after school and on weekends taking turns with her sisters on the gaming console, and directing her energy into something so structured is soothing.

'Having siblings meant there were always arguments over taking turns and who had the longest turn, but we loved it,' she says.

Books, too, are important.

'We got another trampoline and I would go out and bounce on that. I didn't realise at the time it was a sensory thing. I would take a book with me and I would be bouncing and reading a book. I would take a book wherever I went, although I was told it was rude to keep reading when someone was talking to me.'

She also uses writing as a creative outlet and to help her cope both in class and at home.

•

Jess's high school is connected to her old primary school, so it is full of the same classmates – although with a different head-mistress, at least. Every morning, Jess puts on her uniform and marches through the school grounds, trying to push down her feelings about what is going on around her in order to make it through the day. She pays frequent visits to the nurse's office when class gets too much. The nurse gives her an antacid fizzy drink to settle her stomach and then sends her back to class. She is treated as though she is a hypochondriac by the teachers, but the nurse seems to understand Jess's need for a break and to be treated with care. The bored, restless state she frequently finds herself in, Jess muses now, is likely to have been overstimulation.

As if surviving the day-to-day isn't hard enough, school becomes unbearable in year eight, when Jess is bullied by another girl. Backed up by a large friendship group, this girl leads a chorus of giggles whenever Jess raises her hand in class and makes snarky comments away from teachers about how excited Jess gets over the wrong things. It is the kind of bullying that can easily be written off as a misunderstanding. 'We were just trying to be nice, miss.' But when one of the other girls sends an abusive email to Jess, Jess forwards it on to the school, finally able to prove what she has been trying to tell the teachers. It is the first piece of tangible evidence of what is actually happening. It results in a suspension for the offender but does not improve things socially for Jess. Being the person who got someone from the dominant social group suspended does not endear her any further to her cohort. It is a blessing when this girl leaves the school at the end of the year.

Outside of school, Jess attends her church's youth group. It is her main social outlet, and although she gets the feeling the other kids there do not like her very much, she loves it. Every second week they take part in planned activities like bowling and scavenger hunts around the local shopping centre, while every other week is a quiet night in. This provides a level of comfort and routine with peers her own age away from the stress of school. Youth group can be relied upon, and that is worth something. Jess hopes she will be asked to stay on as a youth leader when, towards the end of year nine, she is about to age out of the group. She has seen this happen before with the older members. But while the two other people her age are asked to stay on, Jess is not. Her exclusion feels pointed.

'It was very obvious they did not want me to come back, they had just been waiting for me to age out of [the group],' she says.

This is further confirmed when Jess's sister is asked to be a youth leader the following year. It breaks Jess's heart. Later, when the minister's wife admonishes Jess and her sister for being unable to attend a planned weekend away, their mum steps in to defend them. Seeing her mum push back against the church makes Jess feel safe to break away herself, to close that door.

All of her closest friendships are made online, including her first autistic friend. It turns out her friend's family knows another family at Jess's church, and so the pair are able to meet up. Jess is just starting to acknowledge her own diagnosis at this point, but is still quite secretive and ashamed about it with most people, because of the way they tend to react, which is usually with sympathy, a good dose of condescension and an assumption of inability. Although she still meets with similar reactions today, they are not as prevalent as when disclosing a diagnosis in the late 1990s and early 2000s. For teenage Jess, there are no positive or even neutral reactions. So it is freeing to finally meet someone who gets her, and for whom she doesn't have to perform.

'You don't have to explain, "Oh, I'm not ignoring you, we are just happily coexisting." That is not rude when you hang out with other autistic people.'

Not having to explain the way her thought processes work is similarly liberating.

'With someone neurotypical, I'll have to explain how I got from point A to point B, because they don't understand the connections. And then I have to backtrack and think, "How did I connect those two thoughts?" Because I won't know.'

•

The dynamic at school eventually starts to shift. Art classes run on a cycle, and Jess finds herself in ceramics, where she excels. Students taking ceramics can go to the classroom at lunchtime to work on their projects. The quiet space, full of art supplies and supervised by a kind teacher, is a reprieve from the social hierarchy that is cementing itself in the year level.

School camp is another elective. Where in earlier years it had been compulsory and filled with a lot of bushwalking, year ten students can pick their own pursuits. Jess attends a rock-climbing camp and has the best week of her school life to date.

'Having autonomy and choice made a huge difference, especially when it was something I was actually interested in,' she says.

Autonomy is such an important desire and right for autistic people, yet it is so often denied them or removed from them in ways it is not for non-autistic people – through behavioural therapies or presumed incompetence, for example. School is not the ideal setting for young people to claim autonomy, and is one of the elements of their education that a lot of autistic students struggle with.

Luckily for Jess, in senior high school she is again offered a choice of elective subjects, giving her more opportunity to study what she likes. She also has an English teacher who is deemed odd by most students, but who encourages Jess's writing.

'She was the best teacher I ever had. She was a bit weird and I really bounced off that. She was weird in an awesome way, although I think she was intimidating to some students. She encouraged us to call out rather than putting our hand up. She had a lot of energy and passion, and it was inspiring.'

Jess is one of only two senior students taking ceramics, and she has a great time with Libby, a girl she has known since prep. They have the classroom to themselves and can chat about everything and nothing as they work away. It is a tactile artform, a quiet space and a genuine connection – the perfect combination.

'We didn't get into anything deep, we would just joke around and be silly. I think we both needed that lightness,' she says.

This friendship extends beyond the classroom, and the pair often borrow the school video camera to make silly movies together. Jess edits them at home on her computer. One of their videos is a school tour, pointing out all the dodgy parts of the buildings that the private school chooses not to show to prospective parents. It is like TikTok before social media is even a thing. It feels as though the other students in the grade have come to a level of acceptance of Jess being Jess, and they mostly leave her be. Or maybe, as Jess says, she just stops giving a damn. She has developed a level of anger and defensiveness as a mechanism to deter bullies.

'It was like, "Go away, that's what I want,"' she says. 'I was so used to not having friends and everyone thinking I was weird that I just stopped caring. I never really considered anybody my friend, other than Libby.' Happily, Jess and Libby are still friends today, over two decades later.

That feeling of being unseen pushes Jess to look for connection elsewhere. She is invited by a girl at her school to join a Pentecostal church where the youth services are like rock concerts and everyone is happy to see her. Jess loves it.

'What really pulled me in was [how you could] let emotions out,' she explains. 'They would tell you to talk to God, to tell Him what was on your mind. So I would be standing there with other people all doing the same thing, full-on screaming all of my problems. It was very cathartic.'

Jess sees it differently now.

'They pulled in anybody who was really lonely and vulnerable, and that was me.'

MICHAEL

When Michael gets home from school, he takes off his shoes, drops his bag at the door and heads straight to his room – or, as he prefers to call it, his quarters. His mother, Vanessa, can hear him having a lively conversation through the closed door. Michael has an expressive voice and a knack for impressions. It sounds a little bit like an argument. When she peeks in, she finds him acting out a scene from one of his favourite television shows, with him playing the part of the villain, saying all the horrible things the villain would say. Acting out the scene in the safety of his private space is a coping mechanism, helping him to regulate and let the bad feelings out after a particularly hard day. (It is also a glimpse of what will later become a passion of his – acting.)

Michael *hates* high school. The teachers rush through the information in their lessons too quickly, and then there are the assignments, homework, exams and revision. Classmates are chatting, pieces of paper are flying. It is chaotic on every level. It feels like information overload, and it never seems to stop.

'High school is the most stressful time in a person's life,' he says.

In the junior years, he finds the other students immature and irritating. As Michael gets a bit older, he starts to notice the girls in his classes, but they do not seem to notice him back.

'I felt ignored for the most part.'

Most of his early crushes are of the famous-slash-fictional kind, particularly as television is a huge comfort to him. Michael finds solace in watching his favourite shows again and again, including *Modern Family*, *Spongebob Squarepants*, *The Big Bang Theory*, *Parks and Recreation* and *New Girl*. He also likes to research and memorise facts about actors and celebrities, including the dates of death, from online film and television database IMDb. He admires the beauty, humour and smarts of characters like Jessica Day in *New Girl*, as well as her real-life counterpart Zooey Deschanel. He is also a huge fan of Kristen Bell.

'She is absolutely funny and hilarious,' he says. 'A light in this world.'

Another actress of note is Rosamund Pike, whom Michael admires for her dramatic skills as well as her 'beautiful accent'.

He loves to watch classic television shows with his parents, including *Gilligan's Island*. He is a huge fan of actress Dawn Wells (who has since died), and fulfills a lifelong wish of meeting her when she visits Australia for a fan convention. She tells him he makes a good Skipper.

'That was pretty much one of the most cherished moments I've ever had in life. It was quite a privilege,' he says.

•

I sought out studies on screen time and autism, because I know that so many autistic people recharge by watching their favourite shows or playing their favourite games. It was disappointing – though it did not come as a huge surprise – to find that the majority of research available focused on whether screen time *causes* autism. (Insert eye roll here.) So much of the research around autism seems to me to be back to front. Does screen time 'cause' autism, or are autistic people more disposed to needing that social and sensory break from the chaotic demands of the neuro-typical world? For example, research states that 41.4 per cent of autistic adolescents and children spend free time playing video games compared to 18 per cent of their neurotypical peers. There is some affirming information and support available out there. Autism non-profit organisation Amaze holds webinars for parents aimed at supporting young autistic people with healthy online video gaming. In their article 'Video games and autism: helpful or harmful?', the benefits of gaming are outlined:

Autism Australia advocate Thomas Kuzma said his know-ledge of Pokémon helped him make friends in the primary school playground.

While a lot of research looks at social interaction between autistic and neurotypical people, it's been suggested video games, by virtue of high autistic participation, can also increase the potential of autistic people interacting with other autistic people.

Such interactions can lead to rapport and mutual understanding. A good example is the autistic-only *Minecraft* server 'Autcraft' that has fostered a safe anti-bullying community with clear and consistent rules.

•

Michael finds the subjects he enjoys, like woodwork and drama, and puts his all into those. As the end of high school draws closer, Michael finds something he never expected: popularity.

'As the years passed in high school I began to enjoy socialising with the other students more and I was surprisingly popular.'

His open-hearted nature and positive attitude strike a chord with many in his cohort, and Michael finds he has friends everywhere he goes around campus. He relates more to the girls, and they are welcoming to him across the board.

'Perhaps that is because I am the second-most sensitive star sign, a Pisces, which also means I am nurturing and caring,' he muses.

It is the girls in Michael's maths class who summon the teacher when he has his first-ever seizure. Michael does not exactly remember it – 'I think I might have lost consciousness,' he says – but he will never forget it either. He remembers the exact date and time (4 September, 12.50 pm), and how awful the hospital stay was afterwards. His seizures continue for about another year, but eventually medication stops them and he has not had any since.

•

Having a family he loves to be with at home helps him decompress from the long school days. Talking around the kitchen bench, or watching TV shows together after dinner, is Michael's favourite way to spend time. He describes his siblings Adam and Olivia as kind and funny, which I say must be a family trait. Michael doesn't agree – he does not find himself to be particularly funny.

'If I try to tell a joke it doesn't come off as funny,' he says. 'It comes off as me trying too hard. I don't really know any jokes.'

•

An example of a time Michael makes me laugh without meaning to is when he says he is not a fussy eater, only to start listing an incredible number of foods he does not like – avocado, pumpkin, cauliflower, nuts, tabouli, licorice, cereal, muesli . . . the list goes on. I totally get it – I dislike plenty of foods as well, for all sorts of reasons – but it is this incongruous juxtaposition that feels so deeply autistic and humorous to me.

Being deemed unintentionally funny is something I suspect a lot of autistic people can relate to; other people react seriously to your humour, but laugh when you are being sincere. Sometimes it might be because we answer questions in a forthright and factual manner, and other times it is because our recall skills are so quick. Observations of the absurdity of social norms are often spot on, and yes, autistic people can be great with sarcasm. It is not all fun and games, but there is no humour I find more entertaining than autistic humour.

•

The Theo family eats dinner together and enjoys going to restaurants and the cinema. Michael has fond memories of a trip to Hervey Bay, where they go whale-watching and visit Fraser Island. It is their only big holiday together as a family, because his parents' work and three kids keep them busy, but it does kindle a desire in Michael to see more of the world. In the meantime, his dad tells him all about different countries and the places he has been. Michael loves having long, philosophical chats with his dad about everything from nature to the universe.

'My dad is spiritual. He is full of wisdom and has certainly made quite an impact,' he says.

The pair like to practise meditation together, which also helps Michael to maintain his positive outlook on life. Michael looks to his parents' marriage as the epitome of a successful life, and takes everything his father tells him about how to find a partner and be a husband to heart. He wants to follow as closely in his dad's footsteps as possible, even though he describes his parents' relationship in quite a colourful way.

'Watching them interact growing up, it was like watching another episode of *The Flintstones* sometimes,' he says. 'My mother often reminds me of Wilma Flintstone; they are both level-headed.'

While home life is his safe haven, Michael calls the day he finishes high school one of the happiest days of his life so far. He has a feeling brighter things await him.

'I thought I was going to be one of the least successful people from my grade, but happily it hasn't turned out that way.'

NOOR

When Noor gets her first period, she is really annoyed. Already at the limit of what she can handle at home and school, the changes happening inside her body feel like the last straw. The cramps, headaches, fatigue, and aches and pains are not welcome. What was once her domain starts to feel as though it is outside her control, and her emotions are similarly unruly. Her mum sits her down and gently explains what is going on, framing menstruation as an inconvenience that women have to deal with, but to Noor it is so much more than that.

'Periods! Oh my gosh, a sensory nightmare,' she says. 'I felt uncomfortable all the time.'

Menstruation also impacts her energy levels and her moods. At certain times during the month, she feels energetic and able to focus in class. At others, her emotions seem to have taken the wheel. She struggles to stay regulated, and feels irritated by every single thing her friends and family say and do. Anger comes quickly to the surface, which then causes her to feel shame, and her irritation turns inwards, eating away at Noor's self-worth and self-esteem. And then, once her period is over, she feels fine again. There is just enough time to forget how bad things get before the next one starts. It feels like another thing to keep track of, as hard as staying emotionally regulated when she is hungry.

•

It is not just Noor (or me) who feels like this about periods. While studies in this area are minimal, the research that does exist shows autistic girls and women (I would use more gender-inclusive language here, particularly because autistic people are more likely to be gender diverse than non-autistic people, but this is what is used in the study) experience distinct issues relating to menstruation, especially a cyclical amplification of autistic-related challenges, including sensory differences and difficulties with regulating emotion and behaviour, which have a significant negative impact on their lives. Autistic women are about eight times more likely to experience late luteal phase dysphoric disorder (a severe form of PMS). I track my period to try to manage the feelings of overwhelm that creep in every month. It starts with tiredness and a headache or two. My ability to cope with stress diminishes and every small task feels insurmountable. For about one week out of every month, I feel as though everything in my life is too hard, like I have over-committed and need to hide away. I am not sure how I managed that at school. Actually, I do remember. As soon as I was able to take the contraceptive pill, I started skipping my periods. I did not know I was autistic then, but I knew periods were bad news and should be avoided at all costs. It was about survival then, rather than finding the tools to be able to thrive.

As the voices of autistic people have started to be amplified in advocacy spaces, more information is becoming available to help us. There are pamphlets and social scripts and books written on this topic, including *The Autism-Friendly Guide to Periods* by Robyn Steward, an autistic author from the UK. It is aimed at young people aged nine to sixteen years.

●

Noor gets through her teen years by masking heavily. It means she passes as a neurotypical person, albeit a sometimes emotional and messy one, but it hurts her mental health and sense of self. She struggles with the nuances of social interaction, like small talk, and how exactly to do it.

'I could talk about interesting, intense things, but when it came to small talk, no, I couldn't,' she says. 'It was nice to have one-on-one conversations with people, though; that was always my favourite.'

And then there are the unspoken expectations, like bringing a present to someone's birthday party. The particularly kind or frustrated girls in her class spell it out, and Noor keeps a mental list of everything she should and should not do. It is something she has to run over in her mind before any major social interaction – another reason these are so draining.

'It's like: Oh, okay, that makes sense. How many things did I get wrong along the way, though? I still cringe,' she says.

•

Autism and neurodiversity support specialist Kristy Forbes explains how reframing neurodivergence – or autism specifically – as an identity and culture means we can reframe so much of our understanding around things like social communication.

'The predominant understanding in society is that we autistic people need help with social skills or making friends. And many of us do, that's absolutely accurate for many of us, but not in the way it is sold. Because while our communication skills might be really different to neuronormative social skills, that doesn't make them disordered, or mean they need to be fixed or changed.

'That is what I come to understand as autistic culture. Because there is a whole population of people, and we are seeing this reflected in research now – that autistic people communicate quite effectively with one another, but then when we communicate with people who are not autistic there are communicative barriers. So I think if we reframe the way that each party communicates and socialises, we come to see that it is like two different cultures, with different nuances and body language, and it helps us to understand that instead of there being a "right" way to socialise and communicate, and a way that needs fixing, there are just two completely different ways.'

The social expectations of high school made it the hardest time of my life, and I wonder if it would have been different if

I was a teenager in the present day, when there is at least more of an understanding around autistic identity, culture and community. I have seen autistic teenagers together in social groups, and what I have witnessed is joy. Pure, unadulterated joy. There is no shaming for interrupting, only acknowledgement that it is unintentional, and sharing of special interests is encouraged. It is a beautiful alternative to what I experienced. As it was, as a young adult I understood that it was important to be part of a large friendship group, to participate in all their social endeavours, and therefore to jampack my weekends with outings and events rather than giving my body and brain a rest.

Expectations were the focal point of my life, rather than needs or desires. And despite all of those years of effort, with every fibre of my being geared towards fitting into this mould, I still failed. I was still the weird one who could never quite seem to get things right. And even with all that knowledge and experience, I still noticed the ways I had built expectations around my daughter for a while. I encouraged her to go to all the birthday parties, and to join weekend sport. Only in the face of her fierce resistance did I stop and take stock, realising nobody *needs* to do any of that. Our weekends look a lot different now, sometimes quiet and slow, sometimes action-packed, but always with needs and desires at the forefront rather than expectations.

Kristy Forbes's own high school experience mirrors mine in many ways, and pieces of it feel as though they are reflected in the stories shared here too.

'Once I hit secondary school I couldn't be the grade-A academic achiever I had always been because I was spending so much time learning and adapting to social etiquette for the twelve-to-thirteen-year-old starting high school. Knowing how to style my hair, how to talk, learning how to smoke cigarettes to be cool – all that kind of stuff took priority for me, and that was a survival mechanism, over academics. And so I started to get in trouble a lot at school, I was on a lot of behaviour-modification programs, a lot of conduct programs, and eventually put into isolation. So I think personally my focus was on behavioural issues and mental health, and I never would have brought the two together and thought they were smaller pieces of the bigger picture that is autism.'

●

When Noor feels uncomfortable at this age, she becomes verbally aggressive, hostile and grumpy. She does not physically lash out, but says she gets really 'not nice'. It is part of her impulsivity that she does not yet understand, but it does have some perks.

'This keeps the boys at bay,' she notes.

There are parties, sure, but they are not anything like the wild parties in movies about white teenagers her age.

'The concept of hormone-fuelled teenage parties was terrifying,' she says. 'I wouldn't have signed up to that even if I could. Ours had no alcohol, and only girls. Much more low-key.'

She knows she is straight and not attracted to girls, but the boys at school are not attractive to her either. This is partly because of their personalities and the way they act, and partly because Noor is so unhappy.

'I had such a hard time being comfortable in my body. My dad was this constantly aggressive, unhappy figure who was not kind to me, and as I grew into myself everything shifted in an uncomfortable way that was not talked about.'

Her father, whose parents divorced when he was young, has issues with his mother, and these largely revolve around womanhood and femininity. Noor recalls when it all came to a head.

'It was a storm that was building,' she says.

While most of her classmates have annual beach resort holidays, Noor and her family visit family back in Malaysia. It is a difference that annoys Noor, until she meets a really nice and really cute teenage boy on one of these trips. He is a couple of years older than her, and a friend of her family's. Noor has just got her first mobile phone, so they end up having a secret relationship. While he is very kind, and buys her gifts, looking back Noor wonders about issues of consent, and the fact that it had to be kept a secret.

'I couldn't talk to my mum, and definitely not my dad,' she says. 'I would not want anyone to go through that. But that's just how it played out because I felt really alone and disconnected, and really unappreciated and unloved, and I realise it was natural to crave that connection.'

The relationship fizzles out when she returns to Melbourne with her family, and Noor slots back into her normal routine. At school, she continues to excel at most subjects, but maths is not one of them. In fact, her dislike for maths is so strong it results in one of the very few times Noor advocates for herself at this age. She insists she will stick to general maths rather than going up to advanced maths. Her teachers consider it odd, since she is doing so well at her other subjects, but she knows her limits.

'I am really glad, really proud of my teenage self, who had trouble advocating for everything else, but I knew maths was not my thing,' she says.

In her final year of high school, she is outraged when she is not elected as the school captain. She cannot understand that having the best marks in class does not automatically equate to the captain position.

'I can laugh now, in hindsight, but at the time it was: how dare they not vote me in. Obviously the popular, pretty girl was elected. I was so mad about it.'

TIM

Tim's teen experiences often resemble a war waged between love and ignorance – the love and support Tim feels from his family, and for himself, up against the ignorance of a system helmed by people who seem determined to exclude him rather than make the changes necessary for inclusion. There are many battles, and the strength of Tim and the people on his side mean they end up victorious, but the stress of this period leaves a mark.

From the moment Tim enters his new mainstream high school, packed with thousands of students and hundreds of staff, he feels his autistic differences coming to the fore. Despite the research his mum Sarah put into selecting the school, the reality of that level of noise and overwhelming busyness means his sensory sensitivities and anxiety are heightened to a state that causes intense distress, making learning practically impossible.

The biggest roadblock he comes up against is the way he is treated by the school. Tim's methods of self-soothing and managing this overload include covering his ears, humming and lying on the floor. None of these are allowed in this new environment. And to top it off, Sarah is denied her request that the aide undertake training to facilitate Tim's typing, as the integration head informs her that this AAC method is considered controversial.

'I was denied my method of communication, PAT, and rendered incommunicado,' he says.

Being unable to type means Tim is unable to communicate with people at school, including other students and teaching staff. It is hard to comprehend the level of isolation he must feel, and Tim says it is humiliating as well. The integration head at the school suggests Tim would be better suited to special schools or other mainstream schools, as he does not think Tim is capable of managing the academic work or programs like school camp or excursions, from which Tim has been excluded. In the background, Sarah is working hard to try to make things better for her son. She speaks to advocates and makes plans to access supports so Tim can participate more fully at school. Sarah also facilitates Tim doing his schoolwork at home, but the authenticity of this work is often called into question, as though Tim could not possibly be able to produce assignments of a high quality on his own. It is an ongoing uphill battle, and Tim feels the impact on his mental health. It starts to hinder his ability to love himself.

'Due to the extreme isolation and alienation, I developed clinical depression and suicidal ideation,' he says.

He also starts to act out at school – a personal protest against the discriminatory and exclusionary practices he is facing. In his book *Back From The Brink: Stories of Resilience, Reconciliation and Reconnection*, co-authored with Sarah, Tim writes: 'As the prosecution read out the charges against me – throwing tanbark, books and other objects at people, endangering people using the toilet with my obsessive splashing of water, refusing to sit quietly at the desk, hitting and running away from my aide, and so on – I desperately prayed to be swallowed up by a hole in the floor.'

This behaviour results in several suspensions, and although Tim relishes the respite from the difficult school situation with a legitimate reason to stay home, he also realises that his learning journey has been severely curtailed. Even at home, his safe space, Tim is acting out these frustrations. It is not an easy time.

There is research from New Zealand that shows autistic students are two and a half times more likely to be suspended from school than non-autistic students. Recent research in Australia also indicates that disabled students face routine barriers to inclusion in restrictive practices such as gatekeeping or difficulties in enrolment, segregation to alternative learning programs, and exclusion as well as suspension and expulsion. Students can be suspended or expelled for a variety of reasons, including doing something that is dangerous to themselves or others, not doing what the staff says (particularly in relation to safety) or consistently not completing their schoolwork. There are countless articles and stories online written by parents trying to advocate for more support for their autistic children, as autism is an invisible disability and the approach to support and management varies so widely from school to school. This means that, depending on who is calling the shots, the focus is often on the behaviour rather than the support needs that come before it. Or the 'behavioural management' techniques implemented only worsen the autistic child's distressed behaviours. One parent, who is also an assistant principal at a different school from the one her son attends, writes for SBS: 'At the most recent resolution meeting I pleaded with school staff to look at my son as though he were in a wheelchair. The adjustments that he needs to scaffold his behaviour when he is frustrated or upset are akin to a physically disabled child who needs a ramp or access to a ground-floor classroom. He needs their help, not to be excluded from attending school.'

Sarah agrees that this time was a nightmare for both of them, because of the lack of understanding and acceptance of non-speaking autism.

'Tim was often restless and oppositional at home because of the school debacle,' she says. 'He would punch walls and windows, once severely injuring himself, necessitating plastic surgery.'

This is the frustrating part about autistic traits being framed as 'bad behaviour', especially in settings such as school. This view does not take into account what is going on behind the behaviour. Tim's anxiety, isolation, sensory overload, processing issues and subsequent worsening mental health are all factors at play here, but the focus at school on the behavioural manifestations means that the underlying root causes – Tim's severe isolation and alienation, as well as his discrimination and stigmatisation at school – are not addressed and remain a stumbling block to inclusion. The school, meanwhile, is pressuring Sarah to take Tim back to special education.

To make matters worse, Sarah develops cancer, which she attributes to the traumatic school situation and the ways it spills over at home. She continues her advocacy work while undergoing treatment and, thankfully, things start to change for the better.

With the help of disability advocates, Tim and Sarah are finally able to negotiate with the school for the use of Tim's communication device.

'With more sympathetic and supportive aides and a change in school admin, I was able to complete high school,' Tim says.

'I believe the resilience to keep going came from knowing that we were on the right track,' Sarah adds. 'I feel that every parent would face challenges in schooling when their child is sensitive or has additional challenges, but the support from advocates and social networks, including other parents, has been invaluable.'

Even after reintegration, Tim continues to feel the impact on his self-esteem from the years of struggling against a mainstream system catering mainly to non-disabled students. The lack of understanding on the part of the school – including the administration, certain staff and students – means that Tim becomes sensitised to indifference, slights or rejections, real or perceived. Although he is not bullied, being ignored or dismissed by others impact hugely on his sense of self-worth. At the same time, Tim deeply appreciates some efforts to make him feel included, such as a smile, a wave or a greeting. He views his battles for acceptance as paving the way for non-speaking autistic people to have an easier time in the future.

'I have learned from hard experience that some people may choose not to be open-minded,' he says, 'but, then again, you don't need to bring everyone on board. I feel that I just have to work harder in doing my best, in helping to educate people to understand that we are not from outer space, but have needs, desires and aspirations, like most people as members of the human spectrum.'

LEARNING MY MIND: A DECONSTRUCTION OF SELF FROM THE NOTES APP

Is your phone filled with years' worth of random notes dissecting all the ways you act, think, process and behave, or are you neurotypical? The following has been excavated from the caverns of my device, from before and leading up to my autism diagnosis. To be clear, these are not diagnostic criteria, simply a reflection of the pathway to understanding my own particular brain. I could not connect with much of the dry, deficit-focused, diagnostic language I found online when I first started considering autism as a possibility. I offer this as an alternative. I am not saying that this is the only way to be autistic, or that every autistic person will feel this way. Of course not; we talked about that, remember? It will not resonate with everyone, but I know how much it would have meant to me to recognise my own way of being and moving through the world as autism before I did. I hope it makes somebody feel seen.

- Social anxiety – unable to make small talk, awkward, social hangovers.
- Prefer solitude or one-on-one social interactions with safe people.
- Use alcohol, drugs and smoking as coping mechanisms.
- Dislike physical contact – hugging. A lot of anxiety around hugging, whether or not I will need to hug someone. Sometimes it is all I think about in a social setting – do I go in for the hug or wait to see what they do? Sometimes I stop listening to them because of this internal dialogue.
- Unable to make eye contact with strangers – always eyes to the ground.
- Very serious – can take things literally a lot of the time.
- Hate any kind of conflict – very scared of conflict of any kind. Will go out of my way to avoid it.
- Black-and-white thinking – right and wrong, no grey areas.
- Low self-esteem.
- Anxiety – generalised.
- Very direct – point out people's flaws without thinking about how this may affect them.
- Have a hard time displaying emotion with family. Often say nice things or do nice things because I know it will make them happy. It's an emotional response they may expect. Not because I want to. I love them but have a hard time showing this. Much easier in cards, text, than in person.
- Very sensitive to other people's emotions. I can pick up on them, especially negative ones. E.g. if my partner is upset or frustrated even for a second, I feel it and will ask why he

is upset. He won't be upset enough to want to talk about it, but I keep pushing because I know I felt a negative emotion, and I am so fearful of him being upset with me, so that it turns into something bigger than it should be.

- Strong intuition – sometimes just have a 'feeling' about something or someone that usually turns out to be correct.
- Love for nature and animals – prefer this to social contact.
- Love for education, learning. Quick learner. No issues with education, other than struggled to make friends. Preferred to sit on my own most of the time.
- Have often had to take days off work due to social exhaustion.
- Find staff functions difficult.
- Hard-working, strong attention to detail. I find myself obsessing over the editing side of my job – finding spelling, grammar, layout mistakes and correcting them.
- Struggle to deal if the paper goes to print with a mistake.
- Short temper – easily angered, overwhelmed by my own anger, especially when things are too loud.
- Try very hard to please people, struggle with the idea someone might not like me.
- People-pleasing often to the detriment of myself and what I want.
- Have burned bridges in the past by leaving jobs without sufficient notice because of burnout.
- Have difficulty expressing myself and how I feel. Asking for what I want. Often for the fear of sounding like a crazy person. I know my thoughts/feelings can be extreme and different from those of others.

- Say yes to social invites only to regret it and often make excuses last minute not to attend. This is social anxiety mixed with fear of displeasing people.
- Often mimic acceptable social cues to fit in. E.g. I know to ask a lot of questions in social circumstances to prevent me from having to talk about myself.
- Can write my thoughts or feelings a lot easier than I can speak them – often do this in text, letter or email with my partner.
- Sometimes talk so quietly my partner cannot distinguish what I am saying. I don't realise this unless he points it out.
- Have sensory overloads and need to retreat to a quiet, dark place – this was particularly prevalent in New York City. Lights, loud noises and new situations.
- Big issues with insomnia – my mind can get into a state where I know I will be unable to sleep. Feeling wired, overstimulated.
- Often relate better to children – able to engage in play much easier than engage in adult conversation.
- Grind teeth, have lockjaw.
- Preference for routine and lists.
- Need to be on time – if we say we will be somewhere and are running late, this causes an intense amount of stress and anxiety.
- Intense interest in writing – can engage in this for hours without a break.
- Feel all my feelings very deeply, intensely. The depth of my feelings often tires me out.
- Enjoy movies, reality TV, celebrity for its ability to take me away from emotional intensity.

- If someone says something critical, or I perceive it as critical, I will stew on this for days, weeks, months.
- Easily embarrassed by my own faults, find it hard to let go of embarrassment and shame.
- Often use a different persona as a coping mechanism – pretend to be extroverted to fit in or do my job.
- Strong-willed, determined.
- Operate well in a crisis situation – don't get overwhelmed by emotion.
- Obsession with math and numbers when I was younger, sometimes still today. E.g. whenever I am driving and pass a sign showing how many kilometres to my destination, I will calculate based on my speed how many minutes it will take to get there, then how much quicker I would get there driving 5 kilometres faster, or how long it would take if I drove 5 kilometres slower. This has been compulsive in the past, needing to be done at every sign or I would get very anxious, and is still a habit. Another example is calorie-counting. Can get very obsessive about this but it is more to do with the numbers than the weight side of things. E.g. If I eat xx fewer calories a day for a month, I will lose xx amount of weight.
- Cry every time I read symptoms of Asperger's [note: this was language used in what I was reading at the time] because it makes so much sense of a range of different things I have always dealt with – anxiety, introversion, social problems, sensory overload, obsession with numbers. But at the same time I really don't want to face this, be perceived as 'other'.

INTERVIEW WITH
AN AUTISTIC
PSYCHOLOGIST

Holly Pretorius is the first to admit that a lot of what she learned about autism in her six years of study to become a psychologist was 'surface level', focusing more on outward behaviours than internal workings.

It is not until the second year of her master's degree, her final year at university, when they start to look into the way autistic women can present, that something clicks for her.

'I went and did some more research about it, and my mind was blown. It all made sense, I related to all the criteria,' she says.

Holly describes the process of discovering she is autistic while studying psychology to be an 'up and down journey'.

'I had this conceptualisation of who I was, and I needed to assimilate that new piece of information into that understanding of myself. I thought it was important for me to seek a profes- sional opinion, so I did that, and I received the diagnosis and was very validated and relieved. But then there is that mourning about what life might have been like if I had been diagnosed earlier in life.'

Psychology is not her first pick for post-school studies, but after one year of acting school, Holly realises it is not the industry for her.

'At the time, I knew vaguely that I wanted to help people but not what area to go into. I had always enjoyed psychology in high school and it had been one of my best subjects. I thought that my personal experience with mental health challenges, and empathetic nature, would be helpful for the career,' she says.

'I started studying and found it so interesting. What I like about it is that it's humanitarian-focused, but also a science, so it is structured and concrete, but it's not such an impersonal science. Acting and psychology are similar in that they are both studying people.'

While studying for her undergraduate degree, Holly starts doing volunteer work as a play therapist with a young autistic boy, and that is where her interest in working with autistic people starts.

'At that time, I did not clue in at all that I was autistic, I just thought I was extremely socially anxious, a bit awkward, a bit weird, and had a long history of depression as well, which I think is very much tied into the autistic experience that I have had, and also autistic burnout,' she says.

Even after her diagnosis, with everything Holly understands about being autistic, and with all the empathy and support she brings to her clients, she still struggles to treat her own autistic brain with the same kindness.

'Because I appear to be functioning quite well to outsiders, I often struggle to accept that I have limitations or challenges in certain areas,' she says. 'I get really frustrated with myself, whereas I treat clients in a much more compassionate, caring way, stressing the importance of being aware of your challenges in different areas and having some acceptance and acknowledgement, and putting accommodations in place.'

It is a feeling I think a lot of autistic people would be able to relate to. Holly is also clear about the ways being autistic makes her great at her job.

'Working with autistic people as an autistic person myself is hugely advantageous. I have people seeking me out for that reason. I just get it; I intuitively get it. We're speaking the same language.'

But even beyond her connection and rapport with clients, Holly knows she brings a lot of strengths to her role.

'I am extremely disciplined, I have an incredible work ethic. I think being autistic is the reason for that, and I know it varies between people, but I am diligent and focused.'

With a list that is made up of 95 per cent autistic clients, Holly is able to offer a different narrative from the 'tragedy of autism' that is often felt by families of autistic young people.

'I can be a role model – someone who is embracing and celebrating autistic identity – because kids don't really like to feel different, and other children can be really mean. So to have an example of someone living an authentic and what I consider to be a successful life can be helpful.'

She is aware that it is not just autistic young people who can be helped by her proud and open identity. It is parents too – parents who often come to her at an emotional breaking point, over-loaded with information and fear of the unknown.

'When a parent brings their child in for assessment, I disclose my diagnosis early on in the process. I want to communicate that both my assessment of the individual, and the guidance offered following the diagnosis, come from lived experience.'

Parents, like autistic people, come in all variations, and Holly has seen just about all of them.

'I've had some parents who have already come to an under-standing that their child is autistic, and are just looking for formal diagnosis and that piece of paper so they can access supports. Other parents know there are challenges there, and I think often deep down know it is autism, but almost don't want to say it out loud. So that leaves me in a tricky spot, because I will do the assessment, I will give the diagnosis, and it will be quite emotional, there will be a lot of grieving, and then they don't want to tell the child.'

I ask why that is.

'They are very worried about how the child is going to receive that information, which usually stems from the parents' own negative beliefs about autism. I get quite a bit of resistance from some people, and that is where it is beneficial to share my own story. Some people are open to that, and for some people it's too painful. And I have to respect that.'

When it comes to writing the reports needed for diagnostic assessments, and especially for National Disability Insurance Scheme (NDIS) funding applications, Holly feels the way they have to be structured needs to be improved.

'I really struggle with the deficits-based model. I work from the neurodiversity-affirming paradigm, which is validating and accepting. It is not about changing the brain; it's about working with the brain. So the way I have to write reports is very challenging. It's focused on weaknesses, how difficult the person is. It's really challenging. I always give people fair warning about that, because reading it is confronting. Often the feedback sessions I have for assessments are very emotional.'

She is also wary of behavioural therapy approaches to 'treating' autistic people which were taught as part of her master's degree.

'We were taught about functional behavioural therapy (FBA), which underpins applied behavioural therapy (ABA), so that's very problematic. It did concern me, even when I was doing play therapy while studying; I was already inclined to work in a very affirming and client-centred way. I was never inclined to work in that "this is a behaviour that is bothering other people so let's change it" kind of way. I do hope we see change here,' she says.

I ask Holly to describe some of the biggest issues her autistic clients are up against, and she gives me an insightful rundown.

'I would say the biggest challenge most of my clients are up against is trying to navigate a world which is not designed for autistic people. Symptomatically, this can present as autistic burnout, and other mental health concerns, especially anxiety and depression. Sadly, I work with a number of younger autistic clients who experience "school can't" due to many education settings being unsuitable for their needs.'

Speaking to my own experiences, both personally and in conversation with other autistic people, I ask Holly whether employment is a subject that comes up often. She agrees it does.

'Employment does appear to be an issue for many of the autistic adults I see. Not necessarily finding employment, but the burnout experienced. Some adults need months off at a time or have to work significantly reduced hours compared to their neurotypical colleagues. Within the workplace, many adults are challenged by having to mask their autistic characteristics and navigate relationship dynamics with people in the workplace. Additionally, many workplaces are not very sensory friendly, and they aren't always willing to accommodate their autistic employees. My clients also struggle when their workplaces are unpredictable and they are not delivered expectations in a clear and concrete way. All of these factors lead to burnout.'

Accessing support can also be a challenge, particularly for people who need support but probably wouldn't qualify for the NDIS. For clients who have been able to get on to the NDIS, being able to access a range of support services can vastly improve their quality of life.

'If you are lucky and you get a really good NDIS plan, there are lots of supports available, like speech therapy, occupational therapy, psychology, cleaners, support workers and so on. But for people like myself who definitely have challenges but would be assessed by the NDIS to have "lower support needs", there is not a lot on offer – unless you are financially able to, for example, get meal delivery services, which is something I do because super-markets are a sensory nightmare.'

The accessibility of services is limiting, and often, Holly points out, for people who would most benefit from them.

'It is expensive to access any formal supports in the first place; not everyone has the money to afford the supporting evidence required for the NDIS application. The NDIS is a very inaccessible service for vulnerable people. Even assessing psychologists – the waitlists are so long, it's an expensive service, and many psychologists have limited knowledge in working with autistic adults.'

I wonder if, in her role as an openly autistic psychologist, Holly has had to deal with more than her fair share of outdated or offensive views on autism. She seems to me to be in the direct line of fire.

'I've had a couple of really bad experiences,' she admits, 'which is partly why I am so open about it, because I don't think I have the emotional capacity to deal with people who are going to be really offensive. I'm too emotionally invested. And when I'm invested in something, I can't speak eloquently about it in that moment, or have a productive conversation. So when I blurt out that I'm autistic, often they will hesitate before saying something offensive. It changes the dynamic.'

It is an approach I am familiar with, and Holly says she will temper her disclosures depending on the audience.

'In my personal life, I am not always open about it, because I am worried about that happening. I find with people my age or younger I can be more open, but I'm not super open about disclosing my diagnosis to older people.'

Being able to speak eloquently about autism in those emotionally charged moments may feel impossible, but Holly knows exactly what she wishes more people would understand.

'I wish people understood how much work autistic people do to fit in. Even knowing and understanding what I should do in social situations, I feel I can never hit the mark. That's an uncomfortable space to exist in.

'It frustrates me that there is this onus put on autistic people to mask and cover up their autistic characteristics to make neurotypical people feel more comfortable, and then we are still often ridiculed and called rude and awkward, when we are trying so hard. Why don't *you* try a little more?'

Even while acknowledging all of these challenges, Holly and I still share a lot of privilege. The diagnostic challenges for people in relation to age, race, culture, gender and class are stark.

'I have had many clients come to me for what you would, I suppose, call reassessment, after being knocked back by someone else. And the things that are listed as the reason, it's so so bad. It could be something like, "Oh, but you're married, so you can't be autistic," or, "You can make eye contact." And I would say I see that happening particularly to people assigned female at birth, and adult women will often have a misdiagnosis, which is missing a crucial understanding of who this person is and how their brain works.'

With the rise in diagnoses, I ask Holly how she views people who 'do their own research', and come to a session or an assessment armed with a lot of information. It seems as though this is frowned upon by certain doctors and specialists.

'I know that some professionals look down their nose and don't believe people who come in having self-diagnosed, but I don't see an issue with it at all. And I'm yet to see someone who hasn't been correct in their self-diagnosis,' she says. 'People are experts on themselves.'

As Holly explains, to actually go through the extensive, expensive process of diagnosis, to think about it deeply, and perhaps discuss it with family and friends, there has to be a deep level of understanding required to reach that point.

'The only issues I've had with self-diagnosis are more in my personal life, when I will disclose my diagnosis to someone, and then they will make an offhand remark about being "somewhere on the spectrum" themselves, and will excuse certain less desirable behaviours as being attributable to autism. And I want to say, "No, I think that's more of a *you* thing than an autistic thing." It's almost like, then I can't call you out on that because you're labelling it as autistic, it's removing accountability.'

Speaking of personal lives and relationships, Holly has a handful of friends she knows she can spend time with socially without having to mask.

'Whereas with other people – for example, with newer friends – I have to be in the right frame of mind to be able to hang out with them, because if I'm feeling too autistic that day it's not going to go well, and then there is that shame spiral you go into if you've had a bad social interaction. I find it's better to not have had it at all than to have forced it.'

And when it comes to romantic encounters, Holly says it can be hard for those to eventuate when she needs a lot of downtime. And when they do occur, they don't always go to plan.

'If I have got a crush on someone, it seems to intensify my autism. Because if I have feelings for them, the eye contact is even more difficult, and I am so conscious of not being socially awkward that I often end up coming across way more socially awkward, and then perhaps come across as disinterested, so that's hard as well.'

For her clients, a lot of their closest friendships happen online, which is usually fine for them but not always acceptable to their families.

'Often parents have a lot of concern about that, and want them to have a "real life" friend,' she says.

While gaming and online friendships can be seen in this negative light, Holly is quick to highlight all the benefits it can have for autistic people.

'[Gaming] is often a special interest, it's downtime, and it's much easier to communicate with people generally, online and in written form, than talking to someone in person, because you don't have all of those contextual things where it might be too loud, it might be too bright, the eye contact, the body language, the facial expressions – there is so much to think about. Whereas if you are chatting to someone online it can be a calculated and structured response.'

For most of the young people Holly sees, gaming is a big part of their lives. It is something she tends to support, keeping in mind the need for other things to happen in their day-to-day routine as well.

'Obviously excessive amounts of gaming is not a good thing, but I also think we have been sold this narrative that it's all bad, there are no skills to be learned from this, it makes you brain dead – and I would completely disagree with that.'

Every autistic person Holly sees, and she includes herself in that mix, brings something positive to their relationships. For

Holly herself, it is being a good listener, offering objective and unique insight to problems, and being empathic.

'If someone tells me they struggle with something, I don't question it. I wouldn't expect people to push through; I accept things and validate and understand that, whether they are autistic or not. It is an understanding of struggles. I think autistic people can be really good at that.'

That openness to accepting other people's perceptions and perspectives on how they experience life is something I recognise in myself and my autistic friends and family. What a gift!

Holly Pretorius is a Melbourne-based psychologist working in private practice.

PART THREE

LOVE LIKE THIS

We contain the shapes of trees and the movement of rivers and stars within us.

Patrick Jasper Lee, autistic author, songwriter and activist

JESS

Having embraced an incredible goth style after high school, complete with an undercut, black clothes and make-up, and a piercing through the centre of her ear, Jess is not necessarily what the other young people at her new church expect. She looks, as she puts it, 'unsaved'. And the church's youth weekend camp is not what she expects either. She signs up after attending two services at the church, anticipating an adventure – bonding time in the bush – archery, high ropes, that kind of thing.

'I had been on so many church camps over the years, so I thought it would be like those, where you have a little bit of praise and worship in the morning and then go off and do fun activities for the day, like the flying fox or the in ground trampoline,' she says.

When the bus pulls up at the camp, this still seems like a possibility. There is a gorgeous bush setting, quaint cabins dotted around the site and a central meeting hall for getting together. It is only when the timetables are issued that Jess realises she is in for something more intensive than her previous experience of church camps. There are to be mandatory praise and worship sessions all weekend, with only short breaks in which to eat and use the bathroom.

'And if you didn't go [to all the sessions], you would be sent home in a taxi at your own expense. It was three hours out of the city.'

This approach solidifies Jess's feeling that the church might not be for her. Her doubts about the Pentecostal approach to religion have been growing for a while, and these things stack up.

'By that time, I had started going to goth clubs and was getting more into [that scene]. I saw a post recently about someone going to a One Direction concert and having the same emotional reaction as they did at a Pentecostal service, and it made them realise they actually just loved live music. I had that realisation when I went to goth clubs. It wasn't live music but it was *loud* music and I loved to dance and lose myself in it.

'I'd started pulling away from church because I now had a different social outlet with people who shared my interests. Getting to meet people from lots of different socioeconomic backgrounds and faiths was a huge eye-opener for me too. I'd grown up primarily around people who were white, Christian and from the same income bracket as my family.'

It does not help matters that, upon deciding to stick the weekend out rather than call her dad and ask to be picked up, Jess becomes the target for the misguided goodwill of many of the other campers. They are judging a book by its cover, and she tires of it very quickly.

'All weekend I had little teenagers coming up to me asking, "Would you like me to pray with you?" They thought I was some kind of depressed Satanist or something. I had my What Would Jesus Do band on, and I would be like, "Why? I'm already saved," pointing to my wristband. So yeah, it was a lot.'

It does not take long for Jess's gut feeling that this isn't the right church for her to be confirmed. The end comes in a big, ugly, no-going-back kind of way. At dinner one night, one of the church's youth leaders is asked about the church's position on gay people.

'She opened her mouth and started spewing all this hate about gay people, and I thought, "Okay, there's no place for me here",' Jess says.

By this point, Jess has realised she is gay, and refuses to direct any more hate inwards on the instruction of others. She has carried those feelings for long enough, thanks to her school experiences, and is trying to self-heal, not find new reasons to tear herself apart.

'So that was a big part of why I left,' she says.

Given that she has been consistently singled out and othered at various stages of her life because of her neurodivergent traits, and church used to feel like the exception to this, it hurts. Jess shuts down enough to get through the weekend, with her spiky demeanour deterring other people from hassling her. She keeps a journal the entire time to help her cope with the experience. It shifts something inside her, something unspoken and perhaps unacknowledged at this time, but church moves from the 'safe' column to the 'unsafe' one. The bus ride home from the camp feels like the end not just of the weekend, but something much bigger.

Once she is back home, Jess is contacted by members of the church who try to persuade her to come back, but she ignores them. She does not feel the same inner conflict she did when leaving her family's church.

'I didn't want to make it uncomfortable for my parents, who were still going, so I just said I had other commitments on at that time.'

In the midst of all this, Jess is also doing a film course at the Royal Melbourne Institute of Technology (RMIT), but eventually recognises it is an industry that won't necessarily be accommodating of her.

'I realised that so much of it is social stuff. It's not what you know, it's who you know. If you've got a mate you go out for a beer with, they will recommend you for the job, and if you don't you are kind of screwed.'

Jess also finds it difficult to connect with her peers on the course.

'You know, I had come straight from high school and was mentally and emotionally much younger and more immature than my physical age. I had no idea who I was, and on top of that I had been going to the Pentecostal church, so I had that very full-on thing about religion, because they push you to be like that, and I copped a lot of flak from the other students.'

At this stage, Jess still carries a lot of shame around being autistic, and bursts into tears if she has to discuss it with anyone.

'That had a lot to do with how I was treated growing up if people found out,' she says. 'So for a long time I thought the diagnosis was wrong. A lot of that had to do with how books described autism too, looking from the outside in. It didn't resonate; I couldn't relate.'

Jess quits the film course and starts a baking apprenticeship.

'I had read Kerry Greenwood's *Earthly Delights* series, and I just loved the sound of starting work in the middle of the night when no one else is around, and baking bread. She made baking bread sound like a really nice job, and I do like the sensation of it,' she says.

Having distanced herself from the church and found a more fitting career path, Jess signs up to an online date website and starts chatting to Jesslyn, a young woman who lives about eight hours away in Wollongong. They like the same music and goth style, and spend hours talking to each other online, and Jesslyn comes across as cool, interesting and kind. After a couple of months they decide to meet in person, and Jesslyn travels to Melbourne. Jess arranges to meet her at the airport, but arrives late – her nightmare – because she doesn't have a car and the Skybus is running behind schedule.

'We had both been nervous that we wouldn't feel the same way meeting each other IRL, so we were both fluttery and nervous, and I was feeling panicky about being late, too,' Jess remembers.

She runs down the escalator to the baggage claim like she is the lead in a romantic movie, and the pair crash-hugs in fits of laughter. Hamming it up defuses any potential awkwardness and it feels easy, right from the start, although certain elements of the relationship are not.

'We had to stay at a friend's place while she was here, because my parents were still not okay with me having a girlfriend at this stage,' Jess says.

The relationship progresses mostly through conversations online, and they also start playing *World of Warcraft* together, as a way of spending time together that is not just sitting on MSN Messenger chat.

They fly to see one another as often as they can, which is every few months. While financially draining, the times they spend in serviced apartments in the city, preparing meals together, makes them feel like a settled couple. A highlight is when Jesslyn flies to Melbourne to surprise Jess for their first Valentine's Day.

'That was really nice,' Jess says.

After nearly a year, Jesslyn decides to move to Melbourne so she and Jess can be together. Trying to find an affordable rental property in Melbourne takes some time, and the pair stay with a friend while they are house-hunting.

'[My parents] didn't want us staying there while we looked for a place,' Jess explains. 'They said it would be too upsetting for my sisters.'

Jess speaks about her family with such love and grace, and these days can empathise with their reactions. There is no animosity or anger now, but there was at the time.

'I largely estranged myself from them for years after I moved in with Jesslyn,' she says. 'I was hurt and angry that they thought it was a phase and that the relationship wouldn't last.'

Jess says she and her mum fought a lot when they lived together, and she felt othered by all of the appointments and specialists.

'It's such a sheltered, privileged thing to complain about in hindsight,' she says. 'I was so lucky to have someone like Mum trying to find me the right help, and it was the era, and the lack of knowledge and understanding, that let us down.'

Jess's parents are protective of her, and their belief that her relationship with Jesslyn would not last may have come about because Jess has a habit at the time of being swayed or talked into things by other people. It is something I can relate to, that kind of persuasion – when you are consistently told that your own experiences of moving through the world are wrong, that you are not perceiving things correctly, it is natural to let others tell you how to be, what to do.

'I think they thought it was a phase because I desperately wanted a connection with somebody. I was still heavily masking all the time. I was kind of just existing and desperate to connect with people. So, you know, I can understand where they were coming from.'

When they first move in together, Jess and Jesslyn have to learn how to cohabitate.

'In the past, I could come home from work, go up to my bedroom, shut the door and be on my computer all the time and not talk to anybody,' Jess says. 'So naturally that was what I did. Jesslyn would be like, "No, tell me about your day. I don't want to communicate with you through the chat function – talk to me."'

Jess is also working through some of the insecurities she still has from her teenage years.

'I would get mad if something happened and she laughed.

I would think she was laughing at me, thinking I was stupid. I had a massive complex about that.

'Or, I was very sensitive about my weight, so when she called me cuddly once I reacted really poorly. She meant it in a positive way, but I assumed people meant things negatively.'

Jess also learns what it is Jesslyn needs from her.

'She said, "You never ask me how I am, and that makes me feel unvalued." It never occurred to me to do that; I wasn't deliberately trying to upset her. There was a lot I had to learn.'

It does not take long for them to figure out how to be around one another, respecting each other's space and also making time to connect. They are also quick to adopt some fur babies, starting with two rats – Kiki and Quinne.

'The day after Jesslyn and I moved in together, I decided we needed some pet rats in our lives as I wasn't sure we'd be allowed to adopt a cat and I'd heard rats were lovely pets and very smart and interactive,' Jess says. 'Then we added Lenore the cat after our landlord gave us permission. We've always had pets since we first moved in together.'

This period of their lives is not the easiest, as it is a transitional kind of time for them both. Jess bounces between jobs, and her self-esteem is low because of that. She does not disclose her diagnosis to her workplaces, and does not have accommodations in place.

It is a tricky issue to navigate. Do I disclose my autism, and risk prejudice, judgement and discrimination, in order to get accommodations, or do I push through and risk burnout because my needs are not being met?

Employment challenges are not an uncommon experience for autistic people. According to a report commissioned by Amaze in 2018: 'In Australia, the unemployment rate for autistic people is 31.6 per cent. This is three times the rate of people with disability, and almost six times the rate of people without disability.'

My own employment history is littered with similar experiences, as well as jobs I simply walked away from due to burnout and the inability to mask any longer.

The worst part for Jess is coming home and telling Jesslyn: 'I got fired today.' Jesslyn questions what has happened in the lead-up, what Jess might have done, and it makes Jess feel as though her partner thinks it is her fault.

'It might have been, if I'd been snappy to somebody, but that snappiness would come weeks after not realising I had this stress building up,' Jess says.

Online gaming is still a big part of their lives around this time, as it is to this day, but not necessarily in a healthy way back then. It is a symptom rather than a cause. Video games are not causing her unhappiness – they are an outlet for it.

'My life consisted of going to work, coming home, sitting down and playing *World of Warcraft* for nine or ten hours, going to bed, and then going to work again,' she recalls. 'That is what I did to pretend to be somebody else; somebody who had their shit together.'

A lot of this behaviour is Jess trying to destress after a long day of masking, not wanting to have to think about it too much.

It is a fight with Jesslyn that pushes her to seek help.

'She told me I needed to find a psych who could help me, or she wasn't sticking around to be a target for my emotional outbursts,' Jess says. 'I was also sick of feeling like a fake nothing person hiding behind a shell of anger and rage, when I knew I wasn't really like that. I didn't know how to change, I didn't know about masking at the time, or what it was called, or anything. I just knew that the face I presented to the world was fake and I didn't know how to break away from it – or who I really was.'

NOOR

Stepping onto her Melbourne university campus for the first time, Noor is overwhelmed by its sheer size and the number of people. It is a whole new world, and one that comes as a shock to the system, compared to the relatively small and controlled environment of her high school. As she finds her new lecture halls and classrooms, meets her classmates, and her mind begins to fill with new knowledge, Noor can feel her adult life starting to take shape. This is her first time outside the parameters of her school and religious community, and it takes some getting used to.

'I didn't really interact with wider Australia until I was at uni, and that was probably for the best,' Noor says. 'Even then, it didn't go very well.'

She spends the first months thriving academically, but flailing in the social realm. Friendships are fragile, everything seems to move quickly, and how do you make friendships stick? She finds connecting with other Muslim students to be one way to meet new people.

'I was a volunteer at the Muslim Society – there is always one on bigger campuses – and I felt safer with other Muslim students in our little prayer room and socialising together,' she says.

Many friendships, and romances, seem to blossom this way.

'A lot of people from that group did end up coupling off and getting married,' Noor says.

Noor is nineteen when, through the Muslim Society, she meets a guy who seems nice. There is an instant attraction between the pair.

'He seemed to really be interested in me,' she says. 'But the thing about dating in Islam, there always has to be the goal of marriage, particularly for those of us who were practising. I knew that whoever I was with, the endgame had to be marriage,' she says.

The idea of dating is made more appealing by how unhappy Noor is at home, where her father still looms over the family.

'As I got older, and my dad's coercive control intensified, that just made it so much harder at home, which drove me away.'

She spends time with her boyfriend at university, and marriage soon becomes a regular part of their conversations. It is not really the done thing for young Muslim women to move out of home before they are wed, so Noor mentions marriage to her parents. She is surprised that her dad is against the idea.

'So, ironically, even though my dad was super controlling about everything, he didn't really see marriage as something to talk about. When I told him about [this guy I had met], he said, "Tell him you're not interested." But I am interested, I told him.'

Thus Noor finds herself in another secret relationship.

By the time she is 21, Noor is sure she wants to marry her boyfriend, regardless of her parents' wishes.

'I knew his family, his family knew mine, he met my dad and my dad told him, "Forget it, this is not going to work." It was really dicey, because his parents had overstayed their visas, so my dad was threatening to report them if he came near me again. It was a ridiculous drama.'

And on top of all this social and familial stress, there is the pressure her father is putting on Noor to get into law school. This, he believes, is where her future really lies.

It all gets too much for Noor, and she starts to see a university psychologist.

'The trauma of everything was building up, so my autism diagnosis completely slipped under the radar with all that at the forefront,' she says.

Despite their outward appearance of a couple in love, behind the scenes Noor's relationship with her boyfriend is not exactly smooth sailing. She does not have many examples of healthy love to look to, but even despite this something does not quite feel right to her.

'I wanted to break off the engagement, because it felt like too much,' she says. 'I had this really compassionate psychology lecturer, who was really kind, and she told me, "Whatever you decide, make sure that you are safe." And I remember thinking,

"Oh my gosh, I feel so unsafe in this relationship," but we had already been together for so long.'

Eventually Noor tells her boyfriend she wants to break it off, in a phone call that goes from bad to worse very quickly.

'He said, "If you dump me, I'm going to kill myself and go to hell, and it will be your fault."'

'I told my mum, but Mum was also in an abusive marriage, so she did not know how to advise me. I felt pressured into continuing with it.'

Noor keeps up appearances with her friends and family, but it becomes increasingly difficult as her partner's behaviour escalates. She is not even aware at the time that the relationship is abusive.

'Of course, just like with my dad there was no physical abuse, so I couldn't tell that anything was wrong,' she says. 'And I was too afraid to tell anyone else what it was like. I felt embarrassed – like, I've been with this guy for two years now, I'm invested in this, we've already met wedding vendors . . .'

Just when Noor is at her least sure about the relationship and where it is heading, her father has a change of heart and finally agrees to the union. That is, until a few weeks later, when Noor is accepted into law school.

'I called him, and he said, "Okay, great, now you can break off your engagement because you don't need him anymore – you've got your law stuff sorted." What? It was just a disaster.'

At this time, Noor's father is working overseas as her parents contemplate a separation. Noor welcomes the break from him, but he still exercises control down the phone line. With the benefit of hindsight, Noor can see how her relationship with her father has impacted her relationships with men.

'I was looking for love and affection. I couldn't find it at home so I went elsewhere. It wasn't a great situation, because I just gravitated towards what was familiar, which was coercive control – but even worse, because [my partner] wasn't my family.'

With her father absent from her day-to-day life, and in an attempt to avoid all the confrontation and conflict, Noor and her partner elope. They are happy for a time, but Noor starts to see the ugly side of her husband more and more often.

'His Jekyll and Hyde thing came out. In front of others he was really affectionate, but when we were alone he would say awful things like, "If you try to divorce me no one is going to want you."'

It dawns on Noor that she does not want to have a family with this man. And if she does not have a child with him, it will be easier for her to leave. But it is not until she hits a truly low moment that she realises how bad the situation has become, and what she must do.

'I could feel myself, the depression, getting worse and worse. Until one morning I remember thinking, maybe if I just overdose on Panadol everything will be fine,' she says.

It is a thought that frightens her to her core.

'It was a sign that I needed to go back to my family. Even though that is a wreck, I did have my mum and siblings.'

She calls her mother to come and pick her up while her husband is at work. It is the only way she can think of to get out of the situation without escalating the abuse. Her mum and sister come and help Noor pack up all her things. She cries as she puts her belongings in boxes.

'It was pretty traumatic, the whole thing,' she recalls. 'That was when I started getting regular therapy, which I really needed.'

Thankfully, the divorce is relatively simple and straight-forward. Noor knows this is not always the case.

'That's a whole other drama, how difficult it can be for Muslim women to get divorced, particularly if we are not supported by our families. But I called my husband on the phone when my dad was present, and he agreed. His last words to me were, "Was everything a lie?"'

Noor wants to stand up for herself and tell him exactly what led her to leave him, but she cannot find the words.

'I was too afraid to say anything because I was stuck between two different abusers. It was pretty terrible.'

Now, at 21, divorced and just starting to get some support for her mental health, Noor turns her focus to law school. The attitude of people around her, particularly her father, is that she can redeem herself by doing well professionally.

'You can imagine how that went. My moods started swinging from depression to mania and, especially in the summer months, a lot of bad-boy decisions were made, let's put it that way.'

Noor reflects on how glad she is that she did not die or end up in any truly irreversible situations during this time, and again questions what consent means when someone is deep in a struggle with mental illness.

'How am I really consenting if I'm out of my mind from stress and anxiety, looking for male attention and affection?' she wonders.

While law school doesn't work out, she credits therapy as being a major turning point in how she views herself and her childhood. She is working to understand herself, and her upbringing, with more empathy for herself as a child who was only doing her best. She is diagnosed with bipolar and prescribed mood-stabilising medication by a psychiatrist, which really helps her.

'At least the meds kept me on an even keel for long enough to unpack my childhood and realise that what happened was never my fault,' she says. 'That was a shift for me. Realising internally, "I've been through a lot. I don't need a guy to complete me; I'm already whole. I want to be able to recognise healthy love for what it is by working on myself first."'

Looking back, it is clear to Noor that she carried a lot of shame around her interactions with men and what that meant for her as a young Muslim woman.

'A really kind psychologist told me not to beat myself up. She said she had many Muslim, Jewish, Christian clients who would keep beating themselves up about what happened when they were manic. But you're not well. It's not a moral decision. It's something that is happening in your brain, a trauma. I didn't believe her at the time, but she planted a seed in my mind that flowered many, many years later.'

Noor also credits her faith for keeping her going.

'Suicide is not permissible in Islam, so I knew I couldn't take my life. I couldn't break my mother's heart and those of my siblings, and I didn't want to let Allah down either.'

Prayer helps, and she finds support from spiritual leaders, who help her to understand that mental health issues are real and urge her to continue seeing a psychologist.

As Noor starts to reap the benefits of supporting herself, she seeks to help others too. She volunteers at Lifeline, and connecting with other people who are struggling brings her immense joy.

'It's ridiculous how people say that autistic people have no empathy. What are they talking about? We have so much. That's how we get into so much trouble to begin with; that's the problem.'

Noor works as a teacher and saves up enough money to go overseas with her brother. They go on Hajj, an annual Islamic pilgrimage to Mecca, and it is a transformational experience. They then travel to Jordan to work and study in a community there. It is a small community, and Noor soon feels a deep connection with her Arabic teacher. Their professional student–teacher relationship starts to show signs of becoming something more.

'He was the most sought-after bachelor in the neighbourhood,' Noor says.

But Noor soon begins to realise that this community is less of a community and more of a . . . cult.

'Of course I wound up in a cult,' she says with a laugh. 'Because I love rules and I needed them after all the chaos.'

Noor can see the humour in it all now, but at the time it is a deeply disturbing experience, and she must lean on her faith to get through it.

'Within this cult there were many "Aunt Lydia" types who enforced the idea that if anyone wants to get married, it has to be through them,' she says, referencing a character from the dystopian novel and television series *The Handmaid's Tale*, in which Aunt Lydia is in charge of indoctrination and discipline of the handmaids.

It is made clear to Noor that, despite her teacher's romantic interest in her, on paper she is a 'total fail'.

'Divorced, mental illness, parents separated. I [wasn't] good enough for the golden boy of the cult,' she says. 'He wanted to marry me – take that haters – but I needed to put myself first.'

Recognising that the situation is toxic, Noor flies home to Melbourne. She arrives to find her parents have finally split up for good, and her family home feels safe for the first time in her life. She and her siblings and mum have the space to breathe again, and to start to thrive.

'My siblings and I were trying to find ourselves again, now that our dad was out of the picture, and there was a lot of trauma that was slowly coming out for everyone, and a lot of healing.'

It is a bonding time for the family bubble, and Noor has no intention of bursting it.

'I was really annoyed when people started asking if I had found someone, or if I wanted to,' she says. 'I thought, "Are you serious? After everything I've been through, that's the first thing you ask me?"'

She answers all such queries with a firm 'no, thank you' – she is not interested in meeting anyone.

MICHAEL

Many of the friendships in Michael's life come and go, so the ones that stick are especially important. While he is most well-known for his quest to find a romantic partner, it is his platonic relationships that buoy him through huge periods of change and growth, and teach him the most about himself.

Though they have known each other since she started as the new kid at his school in year eleven, it is not until they have finished school that Michael and Briana's friendship really blossoms. Briana is a bright and bubbly person who finds Michael's unique perspective on life interesting and refreshing. Michael enjoys her energy and ability to make him laugh.

'She is like a grasshopper; she bounces around from one place to another. I think, if she didn't have me in her life there would be more chaos, and if I didn't have her, my horizons would not have been expanded,' he says.

They are polar opposites in many respects, but get along in that effortless kind of way where it doesn't matter how much time passes, they can always pick up where they left off. The pair start meeting regularly for dinner to catch up. Michael enjoys the formality of this arrangement, and they never seem to run out of things to talk about. Briana's efforts to stay in touch let Michael know she is a true friend.

'Maintaining friendships can be hard work, especially when other people don't put in as much effort,' he says.

Friendship can be a minefield, and Michael and I talk about how wonderful it is to find true friends – people who add to your life and make things feel easy when you spend time with them. There are myriad reasons why autistic people might struggle with friendship. Different communication styles, social anxiety and overwhelm, rejection sensitivity and burnout can all play a part. When I think about love as a concept, friendship is one of the types of love I think of first. It can be just as transformational and important as romantic love, or the love of family, although it is not often framed that way.

At one of their regular dinners, Briana drops the bombshell that she is planning to move overseas to Berlin for a year. Michael is sad, but also excited for his friend. Briana tells him he is welcome to visit her any time.

'She invited me to travel halfway around the world for the first time in my life to stay with her,' he says. 'I was quite surprised.'

Michael gets on with life in Wollongong, where he works for a cabinetry company and spends time with his family and friends. Having taken part in Transition to Work, a government program that helps people with disability find employment – working on their interview and phone skills, building résumés and so on – he has finished a TAFE course and found a job he enjoys. But something about Briana's offer sticks with him. Having never left the country, and having only been on a plane once in his life, Michael is intrigued and excited about the idea of going all the way to the other side of the world and seeing what it is like for himself. He talks it over with his parents, who are supportive and help him with planning to make the journey.

Briana is perhaps not expecting him to take her up on the invitation quite so quickly, but is delighted when Michael phones to say he has decided to visit her for two weeks. By that stage, Briana has settled into her new job and apartment, and she is excited to show her friend around a new country.

The travel presents some challenges: Michael is completely on his own, out of his routine, and he has his sensory needs to consider.

'I am hypersensitive. I hate loud noises and loud music, and I need to wear earplugs if I am around it. I also find it annoying if people are in my personal space,' he says.

'It was nerve-racking, but I had to take a leap of faith in that moment – and so did my dad, for that matter,' he says. Michael's dad is more nervous about the trip than his son, but he has faith that Michael will be able to manage.

'My dad told me to keep thinking positive and stay calm as best I could. Being on the plane alone wasn't as scary as I believed it would be. [Arriving in Germany] was nerve-racking as well, being alone in a foreign airport.'

Briana still has to work while he is visiting, so Michael finds himself with plenty of spare time. He pushes himself to start exploring on his own. At first he sticks to visiting places he can walk to, but gradually he grows confident enough to catch buses on his own, to pay for things and order from a menu in German, and to make plans for sightseeing further afield. He soaks up the culture and the history, and is particularly interested in the Berlin Wall, the Holocaust Memorial and the Brandenburg Gate.

It turns out to be an incredible trip for Michael, and one he makes again the following year, while Briana is still there.

'It changed me as a person – I grew so much,' Michael says. 'It made me want to experience more . . . I want to travel more, and not just settle for being a parent and having a job and getting a house. Because prior to that, I was just following my dad's example [of] life. I certainly caught the travel bug, you could say.'

Michael has big plans for future travel. Italy, Spain, England, Scotland, Wales, Croatia, Portugal, Romania and Canada are all on the list. His parents and friends are on board, and why wouldn't they be? As Michael explains, he is not a child.

'I feel discomfort when people become overprotective of me, considering the fact that I am almost in my thirties,' he says.

•

Infantilising, or being treated like a child, is an issue for a lot of autistic people, as it is for the wider disability community. In this case, it seems directly related to how autism is portrayed. One study I read found that nine of the top twelve autism charity organisations in the US only talk about autism in relation to children. Autism is so much considered a 'childhood disability' that some non-autistic advocates who work in this space deny the existence of autistic adults at all, insisting that it is something children are able to 'grow out of'. Autistic characters are children in 90 per cent of the books they appear in, and 68 per cent of films and television programs. The news features autistic children four times as often as they feature adults. It is as if autism disappears after a certain age. The study noted: 'Society's overwhelming proclivity for depicting autism as a disability of childhood poses a formidable barrier to the dignity and well-being of autistic people of all ages.'

•

As Michael's worldview and life experiences expand, his desire to find a partner grows too. He starts to think more and more about what he is looking for in a relationship, and how he might go about finding it. This includes making sure he is always smartly dressed, well-mannered and practised in old-fashioned courting skills, like being able to dance the waltz and the tango. He has not had many opportunities for meeting prospective partners, and his views on relationships are very much in the abstract and hypothetical. He thinks (and overthinks) a lot about love. He has not yet experienced romantic love, but he is sure he will be able to recognise it when he finds it.

'Either you have feelings for someone, or you don't,' he says. 'You have to pay attention to what your heart is saying.'

He does not have a 'type' he is looking for, other than a kind and loyal person.

'The best catch is a person you are very happy with,' he says.

And despite any of the niggling self-doubt he might sometimes feel, Michael knows, thanks to the family and friends who love him just as he is, that being himself is the right way to go about looking for love. He does not focus his energy on masking, or on changing, but only on being the best possible version of himself.

'If you try to change yourself for someone, one day you are going to wake up and realise you are not yourself anymore,' he says.

He sees autism as a part of him, the same as his hair colour or his height, and hopes other autistic people do too.

'That's part of who you are,' he says. 'Embrace it. Accept it.'

TIM

After the hardship of high school, Tim has a well of unresolved anger and frustration he must deal with in order to find peace within himself. He is determined to find meaning within the suffering that arose from the extreme isolation and alienation of being unsupported and unable to communicate. He wants to understand it, and to be able to use his experiences to benefit others. It is a powerful approach to take, and a credit to Tim's strength of spirit.

He writes in *Back From The Brink*: 'In dealing with being different, I had begun my own journey of self-discovery. I have cultivated a habit of tuning into my own internal landscape, examining how my mind and recalcitrant body work, making sense of raw sensations, emotions, thoughts, and detecting the occasional rumbling of some subterranean forces from deep within myself.'

Tim and Sarah take long walks together every day, and this is perfect mental-processing time for both of them. One step after the other after the other. There is rhythm and nature and companionship. They love to be among the trees and wildlife in the local park, and never miss a walk, regardless of what the weather might be doing. After all, that is what raincoats are for. Sometimes they are gone for hours, although time does not feel all that relevant. When they get home they are able to talk about how they are feeling, to analyse how this is manifesting in behaviours and interests, and to plan ways to guide themselves towards calmer waters.

Sarah speaks to this approach in the metaphorical sense.

'I have learned to walk beside Tim and to try my best to understand and accommodate his take on the world, given that he often suffers from sensitivity issues, high anxiety and movement difficulties,' she says.

Tim learns from a range of different authors in psychology, literature and the social sciences. His sister's interest in Carl Jung at the time sparks Tim's abiding affinity with Jung's writing, particularly around facing the shadow self. The shadow, according to Jung, exists as part of the unconscious mind and is composed of repressed ideas, weaknesses, desires, instincts and shortcomings as well as our idealised selves, which we are afraid to take up as we may fall short. To do shadow work is to work with your unconscious mind to uncover these parts of yourself, bringing them into the light.

This support from his sister is indicative of how bonded Tim and his siblings are. His older brother, an introvert, has taken him for bike rides. His two sisters are more outgoing, and love to take Tim out for short trips or to a cafe to spend time with him, and they are always happy to step in when Sarah needs a break from caregiving. This familial love is gentle and quiet, and fills Tim's social cup.

His closeness with his mother, Sarah, has remained a constant.

'Learning to forgo our assumptions and be open to different ways of functioning has taught me so much, and kept us on a relatively even keel,' Sarah says. 'The opportunities for communication are essential, as in all relationships. I am grateful for Tim's maturity and insight into how neurotypical people think and feel as he makes accommodations for my own needs as well.'

Tim's father is an action-orientated type who uses daily activities to help Tim process his many setbacks. Tim credits his 'tall, strong' father with helping him process his grief and trauma around his high school experiences through more practical and hands-on tasks, like chopping wood, composting the garden, and washing and drying the dishes together on the weekends.

His parents' love and support help him to get through this emotionally taxing time. In *Back From The Brink* Sarah writes that the pair believe there is a similarity between trauma victims and autistic people, and I absolutely agree. There is so much that our brain does to protect us from circumstances outside our control, including disassociation and shutdown. It is an ongoing journey of healing for them both, and one that has a huge impact on Tim's mindset moving forward. Their relationship is particularly meaningful since, as Tim explains, it can be hard to maintain friendships as a non-speaking autistic person.

'Because it is very difficult to fit in, and especially requiring assistance for communication, friendship is not easy for me . . . My friendship with people outside family is limited to the support workers who can assist in PAT and talk to me, the number of which I can count on one hand,' he says. 'Most support workers do not stay long as they take up other tasks, such as further studies or full-time work on graduation. So, friendship is very rare and precious for me.'

Tim enjoys conversations with his support workers when they are in his home, and on trips out into the community. He enjoys companionable silence with like-minded people, too.

There is some research around loneliness and autism, and the little that focuses on autistic adults suggests that they are lonelier than non-autistic adults. This is not a huge surprise, given that there are so many barriers to socialising and maintaining relationships. One of the research papers I read observes that acceptance of autism has the ability to reduce loneliness and flow-on effects such as anxiety and depression. Let me repeat that: accepting autistic people can reduce loneliness and the negative mental health impacts associated with it. Accepting – not questioning, denying, mocking, belittling, challenging, manipulating or dismissing.

As Tim starts to carve out a life for himself post-school, he finds strength in his own abilities, curiosity and love of learning. Friendship remains a small but treasured part of his life.

CHLOË

Midway through year eleven, when things are at their roughest for Chloë – when the bullies still bother her and she hasn't found a way to feel *less* about that – she falls for the funny boy in the year above hers: Jacob.

They could not be more different, the neurodivergent epitome of 'opposites attract' that so many of us would recognise. Chloë's sensitivity, her hyper-empathy and her big, big emotions mean she has semi-frequent meltdowns, while Jacob struggles to understand his own emotions a lot of the time, and is more prone to shutdown. Chloë is extremely independent, while Jacob still relies on his family for a lot of support. He loves cars, she loves Short Stack. Jacob likes loud noise and Chloë prefers quiet. He is tall; she is short. It would be easy to go on listing their differences, but in the important respects they are similar: it is Chloë's kindness that attracts Jacob, and his kindness that attracts her. They recognise in each other a kindred spirit.

When they tell each other 'I love you', it isn't for the first time, because they said those words to one another in primary school. Jacob was that boy on the BMX. But playground politics do not get in the way this time around; Jacob has 'grown up' since then, he says – and, anyway, his friends don't have strong opinions about Chloë and nor do their opinions sway his own anymore. As Chloë describes it, dating someone at this age is strange because it is not like they really have their grown, lived-in, authentic personalities yet. They are figuring things out as they go, trying things on for size and seeing what works and what doesn't. Their relationship could be considered more mature than those of their peers, and Jacob is happy that this is the case.

'A lot of teenagers have a new relationship every few weeks, and things are a bit more casual, or dramatic,' he says. 'We were never like that. We've always been thinking ahead a bit more, and not just focusing on ourselves.'

Communication is something they have to figure out, and Chloë recognises she has internalised a lot of the messaging women are subject to around heteronormative relationships: messages like, 'Women don't ask for things directly,' and, 'If he really loved you, he would do that.'

Chloë says, 'It was really hard at the start. I am quite good at giving gifts and I am attentive to people, so I was getting disap-pointed. I've learned that the gift is the gift, not the remembering exactly something I might have mentioned offhand.'

We laugh about gift-giving and receiving as a whole thing,

because the deck is always stacked against autistic people in these instances. Having to mask your feelings when a gift misses the mark is incredibly hard, especially because people seem to expect some kind of running commentary on all the things you like about the gift, and how you plan to use it.

'It's just a thing, isn't it? Like, what do you say? "I like the texture"? But, really, don't expect a certain facial expression or reaction from an autistic person when you give them a gift,' Chloë says. 'Let them be.'

As neither Chloë nor Jacob are fully aware of their own neuro-divergence at this age, there is a lack of context for them both around some of these communication challenges. While Jacob might not know in the clinical sense, there is an understanding around the 'Smith way' of doing things – the way the men in his family like things done. It is a simple statement of fact and one that is not particularly questioned by anyone at this stage. Sure, Smith men can be particular, but that's just how it is and how it has always been. One of the ways this manifests in Jacob's relationship with Chloë is with allocation of spare time, and how they spend it. The couple gets together every Friday night for date night; it fast becomes their tradition. Chloë catches the bus over after school and they watch movies. Jacob spends all of Saturday and Sunday morning with his friends and family, and then goes to Chloë's house on Sunday afternoons. It works for both of them, but Chloë doesn't realise how rigid this shared schedule is until she tries to deviate from it.

'One time I wanted to hang out on a Wednesday night, and he was just like, "No, we can't do that, sorry." He didn't have any other plans. It was, "That's not what we had planned, I just can't see you on another day." I remember feeling like, what the heck, man?'

The pair learn quickly how to communicate directly with one another and talk everything through.

'We don't rely on "well you should have known" or "why didn't you pick up on that",' Chloë says.

After she finally finishes high school (hooray!), Chloë moves in with Jacob and his family for what she dubs her gap year. It is during this time that Jacob's family learn the 'Smith way' has another name, when his dad is told by a psychologist that he 'probably has Asperger's'. This gives Jacob and his brother an understanding of themselves, too, but Chloë has not yet been given this insight into her own neurology. She is still resistant to the idea of being autistic because it has been a constant whisper around her in relation to her proficiency in maths and science, and her social struggles. And because she is so different from Jacob, it does not feel as if she could share the diagnosis.

The year together passes comfortably as both Chloë and Jacob work on supporting their own mental health after the ordeal of high school. But after some much-needed rest and recovery time, Chloë's ambitions start to bubble to the surface. She wants to study engineering, the logical next step for someone so skilled at maths, and she wants to study at a university in Melbourne. It is not a hard conversation – Chloë tells Jacob she is moving to the other side of the country, and he understands. In fact, he decides to give it a go as well, so Chloë finds a share house for them in Melbourne and they leave Western Australia together.

Chloë sees the move as a fresh start and a clean slate for herself in a social sense; she is keen to make some new friends at uni who share her interests.

'I thought, "No one knows who I am, no one knows me as this weird, annoying person."'

She takes part in a first-year engineering camp, where she makes a great group of friends and meets some other women engineering students. A few weeks after returning from the camp, though, Chloë notices that she is being excluded from the group.

'I remember once I was sitting with them in the bar at uni, and they planned an event and didn't invite me, even though I was right there. What the hell?'

The next place she looks for community is in the queer department.

'I made heaps of friends, people loved me, and I realised, Oh! Maybe I was excluded because I am queer.'

As Chloë excavates these layers of self, she then finds the disability department, initially joining because of her chronic pain. There she makes a close friend who has ADHD, and it feels like a light bulb moment. Chloë starts to learn more about what neurodivergence can look like in people outside the 'young white boy' mould, and seeks out diagnosis. After getting a referral for a psychiatric appointment through her university, and a six-week wait, she receives a diagnosis of ADHD and 'very mild Asperger's', which makes her laugh because it is not a thing, not in the *DSM*; it's an outdated term and unofficial levelling system, seemingly delivered in this way so as not to offend her. The doctor tells her, 'You don't need to tell people about it, or make it your personality, it's just useful to know.' But Chloë is not offended. She is not sure exactly when she knew she was autistic, but it was some time before the appointment.

'It helped me so much,' she says. 'Not knowing why I couldn't reach my potential was so frustrating. And my ADHD diagnosis brought medication and accommodations that I really need.'

We are not going to use puzzle-piece analogies in this book, as the connotations are that of a missing piece, or a 'puzzling' condition, but this self-understanding gives Chloë the opportunity to connect with people in more meaningful ways.

'As I found more neurodivergent people, I realised I fit in with queer people because a significant amount are neurodivergent and that's the bit that's missing [with others]. That is why I couldn't get along,' she says. 'Looking at my friendships, there is not a single person I've had a good friendship with who is not neurodivergent. I can't do that [neurotypical] communication. You gravitate towards people who use the same communication style as you, that's pretty natural.'

Gravitating towards other neurodivergent people when you are neurodivergent yourself is a common experience, and Chloë's framing of it both makes me laugh and rings so true.

'It's funny to me the way people talk about diagnoses exploding, and it's a trend because it happens in friendship groups. It's because these people have the same neurotypes that they are friends. All of my friends are autistic or have ADHD. My psych tried to tell me, "You have friends, so you can't be [autistic]" – and all of them are neurodivergent. Then he said, "Your partner?" Autism! I think it's [reached] the point where anyone who has had a meaningful friendship with me needs to consider getting assessed.'

Jacob, meanwhile, has made the move to Melbourne to be with Chloë, but he does not land on his feet in quite the same way she does. While she is busy with university and the many extracurricular activities she has taken on, like advocacy work and being president of the orchestra, it is the worst year of Jacob's life. He finds a job but hates it, and he feels overwhelmed by all the change.

'I had super-bad depression and anxiety, and I wasn't ready for it,' he says. 'We were also living in a share house with strangers, so I spent pretty much twelve months inside doing nothing.'

Chloë is supportive; she understands why he is struggling. We talk about this in relation to empathy, and the assumption that autistic people don't feel it.

'A lot of people say autistic people lack theory of mind, or cognitive empathy, putting yourself in another person's shoes. I think that it's a case of: if I put myself in another autistic person's shoes, I am very good at cognitive empathy . . . but trying to put myself in a neurotypical person's shoes, my logical conclusions are different. That's what is focused on, but when has a neurotypical person put themselves in an autistic person's shoes and got the right answer? Like, if I was overwhelmed in a shop and acting erratic, a non-autistic person is going to be like, "Why would you do that?", [while] an autistic person is going to understand there's fluorescent lights and a lot of noise – so that's another form of the double empathy problem, I think.'

When Jacob is offered the opportunity to move back to Western Australia, where there is a job waiting, the choice is an easy one.

'It sounded good, so I went back.'

Chloë understands that Jacob needs to do what is right for him.

A SHORT ESSAY
ABOUT RUNNING

When life gets too much, I run.

This is not a novel concept – I am sure most people are aware of fight or flight, and its less-succinct cousin, fight-flight-freeze-fawn.

When my heart starts rattling in its cage and those danger! danger! hormones flood my brain, getting as far away as possible from where I am is the only thing that makes any sense. Not that I am even thinking about what makes sense; thoughts are left behind like cartoon dust. *Meep meep.*

In autism support settings, running is often referred to as wandering, absconding, eloping, fleeing or piss-bolting and scaring the absolute shit out of everyone. That last one was coined by me the first time my daughter made a dash for it in a busy car park. I wonder if other people think of this as bad behaviour, something to be scolded out of children. The fear I feel when my daughter legs it is because I know she is not in control of herself in this moment. She is not looking for cars or bikes or people or broken glass. It is only luck and timing and the universe that keeps her safe.

For young autistic people, that kind of flight-style running can have real consequences – I remember the first time I heard the statistic that autistic children are 160 times more likely to drown than non-autistic children, while listening to Autism Swim founder Erika Gleeson talking to Jessie Aiton for her podcast *Life on the Spectrum*. *One hundred and sixty times more likely to drown.* That is horrifying. It is has made me reluctant to ever have a pool, and has led to a hypervigilance around bodies of water that is often read as helicopter parenting. Maybe it *is* helicopter parenting. Maybe I am the lifesaving rescue helicopter we wave to as it patrols our local beach on weekends.

Running regulates, so while there is danger (as any woman who runs alone can tell you), there is security too. Running as an outlet can be life-changing – or, perhaps more accurately, life-soothing. I know because it has soothed my life. Running is rhythm. Running is breath. Running is flattening out the scrunched-up piece of A4 paper that is my mood and finally being able to read what is written there, in my messy scrawl. Most of the time it reads: OVERWHELMED. But hey, at least I know now. And I can show my creased piece of paper to others, so many of whom are under the impression that I am: DIFFICULT ANGRY MEAN PETULANT STUBBORN LAZY. Running regulates a nervous system that tends to get stuck on *nervous*. It tires the body to ease the mind; it puts me in nature, in community, in my body. Running heals.

The impulse to run can kick in without any actual running taking place. I can leave the conversation, leave the room, leave the group chat, leave the friendship. Leaving is one of my very best skills. I left a long-term relationship via email, if we want to talk about running. There was not much he could say to that. A lifetime of masking, and not knowing why my brain works the way it does, left me without a sense of self. I needed to be alone to figure out where my edges were.

Moving back to my childhood home was not a movie-montage moment. It was itchy and uncomfortable like op-shop wool. I had not figured out yet how to be still. And so I ran. Every morning with my dad – the same route, the same hill. The stitch in my side marked progress, up and up, until it no longer came at all. I started to see that what I felt was OVERWHELMED. It took many more years to understand that really meant BURNT OUT STRUGGLING AUTISTIC.

I don't know that I *like* running. I like chocolate and naps and reading the kind of book that makes my heart swell. I hate sweat and discomfort. The effort of it all. I like having run. I like when the effort is over, and the ease has set in. I wish that ease for everyone, especially now, especially today.

Okay, I've got to run.

A LIST OF 23 THINGS AUTISM IS NOT

1. A disease
2. A bandwagon
3. A fad
4. An epidemic
5. A look
6. Mild
7. Medium
8. Spicy (okay, sometimes we can be spicy)
9. Something that everyone has 'a little bit of'
10. Something that only affects children
11. Something that only affects boys
12. Something to train out of a person
13. Something to fear
14. An excuse or defence for committing a crime
15. An excuse or defence for being a jerk

16. Inspiring
17. Tragic
18. Caused by parenting styles
19. Caused by television
20. Caused by red cordial
21. A reason for exclusion
22. A reason to cause a person harm
23. A puzzle with a missing piece

PART FOUR

ALL THE WAYS
WE LOVE

Why should I cry for not being an apple, when I was born an orange, I'd be crying for an illusion, I may as well cry for not being a horse.

Donna Williams, autistic writer

NOOR

Noor's brother – not the one she travelled overseas with but the one who stayed home – is keen for her to meet a friend he has made at his gardening club. He admits he does not think this guy is exactly Noor's type, but might she give him a chance anyway?

'That got my hackles up, because he was saying he knew my type was an alpha-male, confident, toxic, narcissistic, red-flag kind of guy,' she says.

She agrees to go along, partly to prove her brother wrong, but also because she ultimately trusts his judgement.

'I remember the first time I saw him, this guy in the group, I didn't have that bolt of instant attraction. I was disappointed, but I also thought, "This is different. Maybe it's good."'

Noor decides to take matters into her own hands. She wants to be in control of her destiny.

'I sent him a Facebook message, asking some random plant-related question. I don't normally do stuff like that, I would not normally ask stuff [of] a random guy I just met. He thought, "Oh, she's really interested in gardening." He was completely clueless.'

Serendipitously – small world and all that – Noor discovers she had actually met his sister at Hajj.

'She called him after and said, "I met this really nice girl. I think she would be really good for you, but she's going back to Jordan, so sorry, too bad."'

It is this sister who realises what Noor is really up to with her Facebook messages.

'His sister got suspicious, like, "Why is Noor asking him so many questions?" She was on to it and he was the last to know.'

Then, during Ramadan, Noor asks her brother and their teachers if they can find out whether this guy is interested in her or if he is just being a nice guy. They tell her to wait until the holy month is over.

Noor is frustrated; she hates waiting and wants to know for sure whether or not she should be expending her energy on this burgeoning connection.

'Hilariously, around the same time a mutual friend asked me, "Are you interested in getting married?" I said yeah, I was open to the idea, but only if it was the right kind of guy because I'd been through enough. And she said, "There is this guy – I know his sister." And of course, it was the same guy. So I thought, "This is my sign." My friend was surprised at how easily I agreed.'

After their conversation, Noor mistakenly believes her friend has communicated her interest to the guy, paving the way for her to reach out. It turns out that is not the case, and she catches him off guard. Noor laughs as she recalls it. 'All this matchmaking stuff does my head in; there is no direct communication.'

'So I reached out. I was really direct and blunt, and said, "I heard from our mutual friend you're interested, so let's start talking." He said, "I never spoke to our friend about it, but I am interested, thank you."'

Anyone who had found her approach too forward would not have been the right person for Noor, and she is happy that this marks the start of their getting to know one another.

'I could just tell by the way he interacted with everybody else that this is a gentle soul,' she says.

She also takes note of how comfortable he is with strong women, a result of both his nature and his upbringing surrounded by his sisters, mum and aunties.

'His whole family is full of very strong women, so he has no toxic ideas about women . . . He was taught to honour and respect women as they are, not to bend them to your will.'

Noor notes, in her habit of spotting patterns, that her ex-husband and her father both grew up in families where their fathers abused their mothers, physically or otherwise, and neither of them had sisters. (This observation of patterns comes naturally to me too, though sometimes people act strangely when you point them out. What our brains find naturally others regard with suspicion. We must be keeping tabs for a reason.)

In a traditional courting move, Noor and the guy sit across from one another in the living room at Noor's mother's home with a list of 'One hundred questions to ask your prospective spouse'.

'That is the way Muslim culture works, and it is a spectrum, always, but I printed it out and we did it,' she says. 'And it was really nice to hash things out from the beginning.'

On their second meeting, Noor puts everything on the table. She tells him about her bipolar diagnosis, about being on medication, about how much she has been through. 'I really wanted to be honest; I had heard too many horror stories of people hiding diagnoses, and people being too afraid. That never leads anywhere good. You need honesty and transparency, particularly because you need your partner's support during hard times,' she explains.

'I said, "If this is too much for you, just let me know now, because I don't want to get invested in a relationship if it is."

'He goes quiet, so quiet. He says, "Let me think about it," and he leaves.'

Noor's sister consoles her as she cries, certain that it's all over, that he has run for the hills. But he comes back. He thanks Noor for her honesty and admits he did not know much about bipolar, so he went away and looked it up.

From here, things move quickly. At 28 and 30 years old, they know what they want and Noor is sure she has found a life partner she can trust.

They first met for coffee in August, and are engaged by October. Unexpectedly, it is Noor who proposes. She does so over email.

'I thought, "If you're happy and I am happy, I don't see the reason to wait. I want certainty." He was delighted,' she says. 'And I knew.'

He comes over with flowers and brings a ring Noor chose online. She loves this, as the concept of someone else proposing without knowledge of what kind of rings she likes and doesn't like completely perplexes her. They plan for a wedding in January, which does not leave a lot of time for organising. And just like last time, Noor's anxiety spikes as the date gets closer. Only this time, she is anxious for entirely different reasons.

'I kept thinking: What if he gets hit by a car? What if he dies? I knew that this was a good man, he wouldn't abandon me of his own free will, but I got really worried about him dying.'

The day finally arrives and it goes off without a hitch. They have a simple Nikah ceremony at the mosque, which makes the marriage legitimate in the eyes of Allah.

'We really followed the rules in terms of courtship, which was a green flag for me because he was so respectful.'

Following the traditions and rules of her faith makes Noor feel safe. It means they do not engage in any physical contact or declare their love for one another until after they are married.

They have a small reception, by Muslim standards, of about 100 people. It is held in a marquee down by the river, and Noor's friends and family help to decorate it. It is beautiful, but it is also a lot for Noor to handle.

'Even though I loved having my closest people there, my high heels were uncomfortable, I was grumpy from having to smile all day,' she says. 'Now I look back and see it was sensory overload. One of his relatives said, "Well, what do you expect? It's your wedding." That's such a neurotypical response. Just push through, what's the big deal? When you're autistic, it *is* a big deal, and it's a combination of so many big deals that all add up and end up being really uncomfortable.'

Noor and her husband are both glad when the reception is over and they can be alone.

'I could kick off the heels, wash off the make-up, and we could just be together and relax,' she says.

When I think back to my own wedding, I think 'one of the best days of my life', hands down. But what I really love most is the memory. The photographs, knowing that the most important people in the world to me were there, and that we got to celebrate our love together, that is what I cherish. The actuality of the day? It was more than a little overwhelming. I did not sleep the night prior because I was in a new place, and my brain was fixated on sticking to the schedule for the day. My shoes hurt, I had so many interrupted conversations throughout the day I started to dissociate, and I hid in the 'bridal room' out the back for a lie-down towards the end. So with all of that in mind, yes, a day can be wonderful, but that does not mean it is not going to be overwhelming for an autistic person. And both of those things can coexist. I promise we are not trying to be a downer.

For their honeymoon, Noor and her husband drive to a little cottage in the country with a fireplace and a river where they can kayak. It marks the start of an important period in their relationship, as they spend time getting to know one another better.

'It was me finally unmasking. Finally feeling safe. It was also him figuring out my moods,' she says.

It is Noor's husband who first suggests that she might be autistic, long before she has come to this understanding herself.

'He cited hilarious examples, like how I make awkward jokes around death. You mean, nobody else does that? But it was also my continual sensory struggles, stuff that is too bright or too loud, too cold, too hot. And how my capacity to endure physical discomfort is really limited. If I have a mild toothache, that's something my husband could ignore for days, but for me my pain is all I can focus on. It has taken me a while to accept that about myself, instead of feeling like I am weak, or something is wrong with me. I am just wired sensitively. This is how my body is. It is okay that this is how I am.'

Having a partner who not only sees her but holds space for her journey of self-discovery is something Noor is exceptionally grateful for.

'We've been through a lot of ups and downs together, and he is still my best friend,' she says.

They make a great team. But as Noor and her husband settle into their marriage, they start to consider: do they want to add to that team?

JESS

It is not easy, but Jess starts working with her psychologist on 'unmasking'. It is the first time she has ever felt truly seen and helped by a specialist, and Jess acknowledges that it is this particular one who helps her to finally start to heal. They talk and talk and talk in their sessions, like friends working together on a group assignment, only the assignment in this instance is 'help Jess find out who Jess really is under all of this trauma'. He encourages her to reconnect with passions from her past which she may have let go because of shame or what other people would think.

'No one had ever explained the workings of my brain, or why I felt so chaotic – it was huge,' she says. 'Undoing that shame and self-hate also let me feel confident enough to advocate for myself.'

The need for self-advocacy comes into play when Jess is working a new job at a supermarket bakery. She feels pretty good about how it is going.

In Jess's first feedback meeting at her new job, as part of her probationary period, she is told she is doing great. With her history of stressful employment situations, this is welcome news, and one she celebrates at home with Jesslyn. Later, though, she finds out things are not going as well as she had been led to believe.

'I found out that the bakery manager at the time was on his way out and thought it would be funny to say I was doing well, so the store would be forced to keep me, because they can't fire you as easily once you've passed the trial period,' she says.

It is a blow. She hears from other staff that management is planning to let her go. She is called into another meeting.

'At that point I had told the new bakery manager about my diagnosis, but he hadn't told anyone else, so when I got into that meeting, I said, "I think you should know I told the manager a month ago that I'm autistic." And I laid out how every single thing they had noted as a complaint against me is related in some way to how I present myself as an autistic person, such as my tone of voice, my facial expressions and the fact that I sigh a lot. I also had a confirmation of diagnosis letter and my dad came with me to the meeting as a witness, both of which helped immensely. And they stopped the meeting. They couldn't fire me because it would be discrimination.'

Jess's act of self-advocacy sparks something inside her, and she starts to feel empowered.

'That was when I stopped feeling so much shame about [my autism] and started to recognise that I had support needs and that a company could actually support me if I asked,' she says.

It is easy to imagine that a workplace where the management's attempt to fire her is thwarted at the last minute does not exactly make Jess feel welcome. The manager is not happy, as he already had someone lined up to take over Jess's role. But she keeps her head down, joins the union and covers extra work for two other bakers, resulting in a wrist injury that takes her out of the workplace for nearly six months.

This period is a huge time of exploration and self-discovery for Jess. There are so many hard parts, and so many good parts too. She and Jesslyn have been together for a while now, and her family is starting to accept their relationship.

'They figured out pretty quickly that she is the more mature and responsible one of the two of us, and she kind of pulls me into line,' Jess says.

The couple's animals have a huge positive impact on their lives. When Jess brings home a rabbit called Bunford and plops him onto Jesslyn, it marks a shift for all of them.

'Jesslyn has said more than once that seeing that a bunny could love her unconditionally helped with her depression and negative self-talk, and it made her feel happy again,' she says.

There is quite a bit of research about animal-assisted therapy and the benefits it can have for autistic people in reducing stress. I do not think this is unique to autistic people, but I do know that a lot of autistic people in my life have particularly close and important relationships with animals. During a tricky year with my daughter transitioning to school, we got pet chickens and they have been healing our whole family ever since. Dysregulation is down, sleep is better, and confidence is on the rise. I understand that 'if you're struggling, buy a pet about it' is either the very best or the very worst advice. For us, it was the former.

While on sick leave, Jess starts to think beyond the toxic workplace that has made her feel so bad about herself for so long.

'I was thinking, what else am I going to do with my life?'

There is something Jess has always wanted to try, and when the thought pops into her mind she acts right away. She wants to make beautiful, interesting, weird, wild cakes. Cakes that express her creative talents and let her push herself to new limits.

'I feel kind of bad about it, because I rang up TAFE and started asking about their courses without telling Jesslyn [what I wanted to do]. She felt blindsided by it, because we hadn't had a conversation. [But] I was so desperate to find another thing I actually wanted to do.'

While Jesslyn is not happy that Jess made up her mind without discussing it first, she understands the need for change, and Jess goes back to TAFE.

Her new schedule gives her more time to work on unpacking all of the negative beliefs she has about herself, and to learn more about autism and autistic pride. A lot of this learning is done online, as well as with her psychologist.

'The big difference with what you read online is that it is coming from inside,' she says.

Her psychologist also helps her with something that has confused her for years. 'I was saying to him that people tell me I'm angry and in a bad mood when I'm not at all,' she says.

The psychologist explains that people might think she is angry when she talks because she is tense all the time, particularly in her neck and jaw.

'It was stuff I had got into trouble for at work: "Stop putting everyone in a bad mood." For so long I had no idea what that was about.'

What it is about is that Jess has suffered tension pain in her jaw for most of her life, and her colleagues were reading that physical tension as an 'unhappy expression' and thinking Jess was in a permanent bad mood. It is something I relate to. My tension pain ends up in my shoulders rather than my jaw, and often means I look anxious and stressed, shoulders under my ears. The tricky thing is, that kind of physical tension can trigger mental anxiety because your body is reading those cues as well. Ah, the joys of being autistic.

After completing her pastry course, Jess starts working at a high tea place and making decorative cakes on the side, but she is fired after the busy Christmas period and returns to the super-market. In her role as an emergency baker, she works in other stores and realises that the toxic culture does not exist everywhere.

'I realised, hey, there are actually stores out there that aren't toxic, so I ended up going back to that full-time, while still exploring different hobbies like cake decorating,' she says. 'I also realised that I couldn't make cakes full-time or I would burn out, [and] that being able to make them in my own time made it a joyful experience instead of having to churn them out to make enough money to live on.'

With all the self-knowledge she has acquired, Jess sees a huge change in how she handles herself in her job.

'I remember one day where I could feel myself getting worked up, and I could say to myself, "Well, you're getting worked up because this oven is noisy, and there are other screechy noises in the background, and if you can just hold on until you get home, it will be okay, it will be quiet there." I still remember it now; that was a real moment of clarity for me, like something I had never accommodated and allowed for myself before. I had just let these things build up and up.'

Jess and Jesslyn ride this energy of self-discovery to a completely new place when they develop a new shared interest together – one that involves stepping *way* outside their comfort zones.

CHLOË

Chloë and Jacob begin a long-distance relationship, but it does not feel as hard or as strange as people make it out to be.

'We knew we always wanted to be together so long distance was not a huge deal in the scheme of things,' Chloë says. 'We talked when we talked, and we didn't when we didn't. We messaged each other, but it wasn't like we were video calling every night,' she says.

Jacob agrees. 'We were always thinking of each other, but we didn't spend all day moping about it,' he says. 'I earned money, I grew up a bit, I got on my medication, and I was fine.'

They see each other at Christmastime, and a couple of other visits throughout the year. These are usually well planned, so when Jacob calls Chloë one weekend to ask what she is doing the following Friday, she is annoyed at the short notice.

'It was this back and forth, where I was like, "You can't just barge in and expect me to be available and not give me any details. I have a life to live."'

That seems to end the conversation, and Chloë soon forgets about it. She goes clubbing with her friends on Thursday night, gets home at a silly hour in the morning, and is woken a few hours later to find Jacob in her room.

'I think, "Am I hallucinating? What is going on?" He just stood there and said, "Will you marry me?" I said, "Yes, but also, what the heck?"'

It is probably the only time Jacob has been able to surprise Chloë without her figuring out he is up to something. He has coordinated it with her housemates and pulled it off without a hitch. He also brings her favourite Western Australian treat, spearmint milk.

'It was really special,' Chloë says. 'It was so funny, though. I then had to go into uni and spend eight hours in the computer lab modelling a bridge.'

After three years of long distance, including the romantic proposal, the couple are reunited when Jacob has another go at living in Melbourne in January 2020. This time, they decide to get a place together, just the two of them.

'I was fine; I was excited for it instead of crying,' Jacob says, comparing this move to his first attempt.

'He's grown so much since moving to Melbourne,' Chloë says.

'Yeah, I've put on about fifteen kilos,' he replies.

Their commitment to each other, and to open communication, has laid the groundwork for a relationship that has successfully transitioned from teen years to adulthood. I find it hugely inspiring, and not in the inspiration porn kind of way.

If you haven't heard it before, the incredible Stella Young, a late disability advocate and icon, coined the term 'inspiration porn' to describe how disabled people are often objectified to make non-disabled people feel better about themselves. In an online article for the ABC program *The Drum*, she wrote:

Let me be clear about the intent of this inspiration porn; it's there so that non-disabled people can put their worries into perspective. So they can go, 'Oh well if that kid who doesn't have any legs can smile while he's having an awesome time, I should never, EVER feel bad about my life'. It's there so that non-disabled people can look at us and think 'well, it could be worse . . . I could be that person'.

In this way, these modified images exceptionalise and objectify those of us they claim to represent. It's no coincidence that these genuinely adorable disabled kids in these images are never named: it doesn't matter what their names are, they're just there as objects of inspiration.

So, not like that.

Jacob also times his move well in that he is able to get a job before the pandemic hits. Having worked in food production, which he says is horrible, Jacob lands his dream job at an iconic car company, where he works on converting American cars to right-hand drive for the Australian market.

'It's a company I've loved for a long time, so it's pretty cool to work for them,' he says.

Chloë is thrilled to no longer be living in a share house, and happy that she isn't alone during Melbourne's extensive lockdowns.

'Us moving in together was great,' she says. 'If I had been in a share house in a pandemic, I don't know how I would have coped with my bedroom being my only space.'

Getting used to living together again, and to all the work that comes with running a household, has not all been easy. Chloë has set up their routine with chores on an app, and they have signed up for a meal delivery service.

'It was taking up too much time and energy to plan all the meals, make an ingredient list, go shopping, put everything away, and then when you go to make the food you have to get everything out and measure things. There are too many steps,' Chloë says.

'It's nasty,' Jacob agrees.

Struggles with executive functioning are common for autistic people. Executive functioning is a concept related to the particular brain functions necessary to perform tasks. Examples include the ability to effectively manage one's time, plan ahead and organise, and carry out activities with multiple steps. Like Chloë and Jacob, I too find meal planning very challenging.

Living together means the pair spend a lot of incidental time together, and we talk a bit about what it means to have 'shared interests' versus shared values and ideals.

Jacob says they are very different. 'We do a lot of things on our own. Do normal couples spend all their time together? Is that a thing? We do spend a bit of time together.'

I am not able to answer this question about hypothetical 'normal' couples. Who knows?!

Chloë says they try to have one meal a day together, and they will spend a lot of time in the same room while both on their computers.

'We'll send each other TikToks or call out and interact,' she says.

Chloë is not much of an animal person, but she loves sending duck videos to Jacob to hear him laughing from another room.

'That's the best,' she says.

'Ducks are so quacky,' he adds.

They like to do Lego together, whenever they can afford a new set, and Chloë lets Jacob open any parcels that arrive, because he loves it so much.

Chloë does her best to show an interest when Jacob talks about cars, but it's hard if he is trying to explain something at night-time, when her ability to focus is at its lowest.

'When I can focus, I do listen to him explain bits about cars,' she says.

'It doesn't go in, though, does it?' Jacob asks.

'Some of it does. Like, you said when it's really hot and your engine is overheating you put the heater on in the car to help the engine cool down.'

'Oh, you remembered! Good job.'

Chloë works in advocacy now, and she has a better grasp of the more affirming language and current understandings of autism. She teaches Jacob, and me, a lot about autistic pride and culture.

'Jake has alexithymia, so he doesn't understand a lot of his emotions, and I try to help him understand them and process them. Like, "Are you feeling this way because of this?" Because the physiological part of feeling a feeling is happening, but the brain part isn't telling him what is going on,' she explains.

'I have a hard time tapping into my feelings, it doesn't come naturally at all,' Jacob agrees.

There is a stereotype of a certain type of autistic man, the 'emotionless Aspie', and Chloë says she experienced firsthand how dialogue around relationships with these men can be framed in really harmful, negative ways.

'I was once on one of those awful Facebook groups, purely for curiosity's sake – I think it was "Wives of Asperger's husbands", or something like that – where they complain about them. And they would say things like, "I told my partner I didn't want anything for my birthday and he got me nothing. He is so thoughtless." It was just constant, constant, constant. I was like, "What if you just told him you wanted something? And then he could get it." Some of their husbands' behaviour was shitty, but if, for example, your husband is having a meltdown at a family gathering and has to leave the room, that's not abusive.'

Chloë wonders if people looking in would think she supports Jacob a lot, without realising how much he also helps her.

'I would struggle without him,' she tells me.

'Aw, that's nice,' he says.

I speak to the couple a few days after Valentine's Day, and it is impossible to miss the bunch of roses on the table behind them. It is the size of a four-year-old child. Jacob says he asked Chloë if she wanted flowers, and she said she did. He bought the biggest bunch in the shop.

'The shop was full of stressed-out husbands and boyfriends, and I just wanted to get the flowers and get out,' he says.

In not comparing themselves to other, neurotypical couples, they are able to truly embrace their autistic joy.

'We have a lot of fun that maybe neurotypical couples don't, really. You know, there's this stereotype of the childish joy autistic people can still hold on to, and I think we can find that. Like for Easter I will still do an Easter Egg hunt for Jacob, and make a big thing of wrapping presents to put under the tree at Christmas, because I really enjoy doing that, and Jacob gives me incredible reactions when I do. Just little joyous moments like that. We also echo each other, like whatever echolalia we have picked up for the day we will bounce back and forth,' says Chloë.

'We are very annoying,' Jacob says, laughing.

Echolalia is defined by the repetition of others' noises, words and phrases, but I do not agree with the textbook description of this as meaningless. That feels like one of those outside-looking-in interpretations. Echolalia is comforting, it helps me process, and is a different form of communication, but not a lesser one.

The couple agree they cannot imagine being in a relationship with a neurotypical person, because of the level of understanding and shorthand they have with one another.

'I talk to my friends at work about their relationships, and it seems a whole lot of mind-reading is meant to be happening,' Jacob says. 'We don't have that. We just talk about things. It's really weird that people don't.'

It does mean that their communication styles can be misunderstood from the outside, and Chloë says friends have commented on how rude she is to Jacob.

'My friend and I were trying to watch a movie and it wasn't working, so I was calling up the stairs to Jacob, "Can you make it work? Can you fix it?" So he set up all the IT stuff for me. My friends think maybe I'm bossing him around. My mum does too – she will say, "Stop bossing the poor boy around", but it's just how we are. I think Jake appreciates the direction.'

'Very much,' he says.

Chloë's understanding of autism means she is able to share a lot of knowledge with Jacob, and has helped him foster a sense of pride in his identity.

'Being able to explain things to him – like, you're not an unempathetic robot, you just process things differently, you show empathy differently – I think that's pretty special,' she says.

Jacob agrees. 'Feeling pride is really nice.'

MICHAEL

Unlike most people, autistic or not, Michael has his first date on national television. It is an experience that a lot of people would find overwhelming, but he takes it in his stride.

'It was easy for me to be on camera,' he says. 'I enjoyed it.'

He prepares for the date with the help of his family and a relationship coach employed by the producers of *Love on the Spectrum*. He has purchased a pair of 'love ducks' for his bedroom to help attract a partner, and has such strong views on what a relationship will bring to his life that I wonder if this has become one of his special interests. Perhaps planning his hypothetical future relationship down to the details reduces the anxiety of not being in control of the unknowns that come with putting yourself out there.

'I was raised with old-school values,' he explains. 'I want to meet a beautiful, loving woman with a warm heart who comes from a good family. They are hard to find these days.'

It is clear that Michael's parents' relationship is a huge inspiration to him. He looks to them as role models in how to treat a partner, how to compromise and how to raise a family, which is something he wants to do one day. Their support and contribution during this time play a huge part in ensuring he gets through it all with his head screwed on straight.

•

On the night of his first date with Amanda, Michael is ready. He dresses sharply in a nice suit, brings his date a flower, and arrives punctually at the restaurant where their date is to be filmed. I watched this date unfold with the rest of Australia, and then the world, when the show was picked up by Netflix. I wonder if my reaction to it is distinctly autistic. Michael's behaviour on the date is that of a perfect gentleman – he is kind, considerate and thoughtful. Unfortunately, due to the formal nature of the occasion, his date has an anxiety attack and leaves early. Michael's first instinct is to assume he has done something wrong, like asking too many questions. I do not think anyone watching would agree with this assessment, but I understand that reflex to take on blame in my bones.

When your experience of moving through the world is not the dominant one, you are told again and again, in countless ways, that your perceptions are wrong. This can be in relation to sensory things, like 'that isn't too loud', 'I don't know what you're complaining about, I can't smell anything' or 'the lights are fine'. I feel as though society has a better understanding of this element of autism than on how being viewed as socially deficient can impact someone over the course of a lifetime. Being told you are reacting wrong, feeling wrong, interpreting wrong affects your faith in your own ability to navigate the emotional landscapes of any kind of relationship. Assumed fault at every turn does nothing good for self-esteem or sense of self. I ask Michael about his self-esteem, and he says it is a work in progress.

Ever the optimist, Michael handles this dating experience well and focuses on moving forward. He has another date on the show, with a young woman called Heather, and that results in further dates. They even meet each other's families. But away from the show, the relationship does not develop. Michael says they were not the right fit, and the timing did not work in their favour. With no outside perspective on what dating is like, it is hard to know how much of the experience is tricky because it is being filmed, and how much is just because dating itself can be hard. He is unsure about whether or not he would partake in a third series of *Love on the Spectrum*, if it transpired.

'I am pursuing other interests, with my podcast and acting, and I am focusing a bit more on myself right now,' he says. '*Love on the Spectrum* was the catalyst for a lot of changes in my life.'

His experience on the show gives Michael a new perspective. He wants more for himself than to be stuck in this place of 'waiting' for love to happen to him. It is not something he can control, and he does not want to feel like his life is half-lived.

'My perspective on success used to be that it was getting married, having kids, buying a house, having a pet. A domestic life. Now I see there are other ways to be successful.'

As he starts to imagine what kind of life he could make for himself, he realises there are other paths to aspire to.

'Sometimes things don't go exactly according to plan, and that's okay too,' he says. 'I haven't given up the quest for love; I am simply putting it aside for the time being, while I focus on other important things.'

For people who might have a similarly fixed view of the kind of relationship they want in their life, Michael has some words of wisdom: 'My advice is "trust your gut and follow your heart". I certainly do and now I'm excited, even though I don't know what the future will hold.'

A LONGER ESSAY
ABOUT DIAGNOSIS,
PREGNANCY AND
PARENTING

I receive my autism diagnosis in February and am pregnant by July. One is part of the five-year plan, the other very much not. When it comes to motherhood, the internet has all the answers. You want to know how to tell Braxton Hicks from real contractions, or what labour is going to feel like, really? There are forums and blog posts and studies for that. When you type 'autism' and 'childbirth' into a search engine, though, there isn't a lot about how one relates to the other. You are more likely to find studies about whether birth trauma causes autism, or how soon after birth you are able to spot the signs your child might be autistic. Autistic mothers don't exist, not really. The term 'autism mum' isn't even for us. So it is hard to know how to be. As someone who has spent a lifetime wishing myself invisible, this is not what I meant.

The first obstacle is that in the eyes of many – well-meaning friends and nosy strangers, online 'experts' and even some medical professionals – the existence of one negates the other. How could I be autistic when I have a job, a Twitter profile, a partner and now a baby on the way? To me that sounds like: How could I be hungry when I also have a bike?

•

The autism diagnosis is straightforward (though not quick or inexpensive): a psychologist assesses me and gives me an answer. The amount of reading I have done on the topic prior to my assessment is probably indicative of the result, but it still hits my body in that physical way when the psychologist says yes, you are autistic, no, you are not broken or wrong. In a movie, probably written by a non-autistic writer, with me being played by a non-autistic actor, I would hug her. She has delivered truly transformational news, this softly spoken woman in an office we have rented by the hour. But what I want in this moment, perhaps more than I have wanted anything else leading up to this point, is not to be here anymore. I no longer wish to be seen: not by the kind doctor, not by anyone. I want to have control of when I am observed, for how long, and who is doing the observing. I want to click my fingers and cease to exist in my physical form, whenever and wherever I choose. The bigger the feeling, the less I wish to be perceived. It is called shutdown, I have learned, and it is nothing new. 'Don't look at me,' I often screamed as an injured or humiliated child. I retreated, sometimes to my bedroom, other times further still into the wardrobe, as the room itself was too cavernous a space. It is an affront to be witnessed against my will. I want to be left to deal with my pain away from wide eyes. I want to step out of my feet, leave them in my shoes and take this aching somewhere private. It is for no one else but me.

Invisibility is not a skill I have acquired between childhood and this assessment, so instead I complete the social checklist of goodbyes, thank yous and talk-to-you-soons, and leave. It will take more than five years to process this information about myself, to put on the autism lens (I imagine heart-shaped sunglasses) and take another look at the preceding 27 years, but I don't know this yet. I would probably be terrified if I did. Instead, life goes on much as it did, and entirely changed.

Memories auto-play like the ads on YouTube no one wants to watch, volume and emotion dialled all the way up. Tears spring to my eyes at the grocery shop as I remember the anxiety and panic of arriving at a friend's house to find her already playing with somebody else. I hid in a room to try and calm down, and her mother admonished me for acting 'selfish and spoiled'. Now I recognise I was struggling to cope with an unexpected change in plans. There are so many of these micro traumas, and woven together they cover a lot of mental ground. It happens quickly, and then begins to slow, from minutes, to hours, then days and weeks. Remember when you did this, and how you got in trouble for that? Remember how hard it was to figure out what you had done wrong, remember how hard you tried to get things right? It is therapy, in a way, the kind of work you have to push through. I shed shame like a snakeskin, again and again.

My old life and new understanding of self are on separate lines. It does not occur to me to wait until the work is done on one track to begin something new on the other. I might not fully grasp everything it is to be autistic, to be autistic and a woman, to be autistic and a mother, but that feels irrelevant. I don't know what I don't know. Where there is a plan, and where it is humanly possible, I stick to it. I become pregnant in the first month of trying, but it still feels as though it has taken too long. With a brain like mine, a lot of things feel this way.

There is one blissful week after I find out, and I spend it eating steak and chips at the pub nearly every day. Propped up at a bar table en route from the pokies to the ATM, I daydream of our new life. I tell myself 2015 will be a year of transformation. I balance the eventful first half of the year by spending the whole of the second half in bed, vomiting more than one would imagine was physically possible. I am so violently sick the blood vessels around my eyes burst, framing them with these new red freckles, and so often the enamel on my teeth erodes. They are coarse under tongue, like the pieces of driftwood I mistake for stones on the beach. Hyperemesis gravidarum, the doctor says. I don't say a lot for the next eight months.

Horrific current events have always acted as signposts in my life. It is how I mark the passing of time; I couldn't tell you why. I start high school in the same year as 9/11. The woman with red hair and a kind face is murdered by her husband the year I marry mine. In the haze of dehydration, malnutrition and nonetheless continuing gestation, I have none of these morbid markers. I don't exist. My body fades away as my stomach expands, and my mind feels suspended in this sunken place. Waking is more effort than it is worth. I would give everything I own and everything I am to sleep the time away. I struggle to sleep at all.

With the first contraction, my retreat is swift, from the surface where I meet my eyes and my mouth and my skin to somewhere deeper. Autistic shutdown. Invisible. I cannot embody myself and endure this pain, so I leave my form where it stands. Outwardly, I am constrained. My breathing is ragged and I cannot be still, but that's it, and it is barely anything.

The memory has faded now, and it is only in dreams I recall the intensity with which my body breaks open. Childbirth electrocutes every one of my senses. It feels more likely I will die than survive. And if I do survive, piecing myself back together is as conceivable as reconstructing shattered glass. To be optimistic, I could say I transcend the pain. I rise above it. But it is more truthful to say I sink like a stone, a real one this time, to discover previously unexplored depths of the indigo blue.

When my daughter is born, she is unaware of the fact as her caul is intact. Wrapped safe in her bubble, a sailor's talisman, she is not quite ready to be here. I, meanwhile, am surprised to find I am still in the room. The unlit candles, the unread affirmation cards, the untouched playlist – they have more of a presence here than me. Hours have passed since I last inhabited my body, but a silent baby is enough to bring me back. Fear hurries the moment. She finds her voice once the cool air hits her skin, and it occurs to me there could be pain in this.

Like ice on the exposed nerve of a tooth. Like sandpaper on an eyelid's delicate skin. Like all the ways in which the world is entirely too much. What have I done? A lifetime bearing witness to her pain is unconscionable; I have gravely misjudged my own ability to cope. With this bundle on my chest, I will my mind to suppress the memories of what my body has been through so there is space to process what is yet to come.

I have a high threshold for pain, my midwife says. That can't be right. It has never felt lower. And how could I be better at tolerating pain when I am less able to cope with everything else? I am not known for my coping abilities. This 'threshold' is common for autistic people, I have read. But I wonder. Is the threshold the point where I start to experience the pain, or to show it? And if my threshold is high, does that mean I can bear more pain than others? That I should?

Once she is here, this baby won't allow for any shirking or sinking. There is nowhere to inhabit other than the place that feeds her, holds her, rocks her and calms her. To eat freely again is as close to euphoria as I could imagine on a wet Sunday afternoon, crumbs dropping in the sink and on her perfect round head. Food fortifies me against whatever havoc unbalanced hormones might wreak. Well, sometimes. And sometimes I have to dig my nails into the softness of my thighs to endure another minute of skin on skin, touch that can turn from intimate to intolerable in a matter of seconds.

To be a mother is to be present; your presence is implicit. There are no awards for showing up, only penalties for the times you fail. I tally my own mother's demerits through childhood, clutching them tight like prize tickets I will one day cash in. Only, the pay-off comes in these early months, when I realise just how much of herself my mother has given. These grievances I hold have lost their value. My entire understanding of currency is changed.

As more is required of me in this new role, I come to understand I am at times too present, and others not present enough. My brain is wired for extremities, and on reaching one it retreats to the other. When she cries, it is all I can hear, all I can taste, until I am able to help her settle. Her dad takes her for drives sometimes, and I can sense it in my particles if she is still crying on their return, long before the car door opens and I receive auditory confirmation. This makes being anything other than a mother difficult for longer than it might take those with brains as described on the box. My concentration is singularly focused, and when I reach burnout I need more time in bed than others too. The implications echo in the periphery of my mind: my baby is too attached, too reliant, too used to me being there. Motherhood, much like the neurotypical world, doesn't feel like it fits. But I come to know we are both doing the best we can, this small person and me. We are out on our own; invisible, perhaps, but together.

It is more comfortable to bring parenting into autistic spaces than to bring autism into parenting spaces, but neither nurtures both identities as much as I would like. These two things were always going to be intertwined – how could they not be? – but all the more so for arriving in the same calendar year.

I can mask and muddle through, and I do, but it begins to feel like another way of making myself unseen. And as this small person grows, like a strawberry plant she throws out an arm and suddenly a whole new patch of her exists where it wasn't before. I don't want to model disguise. Small acts of resistance bloom where I wouldn't expect them. 'She doesn't like hugs; how about a high-five?' 'We don't do big parties; how about a play date?' And: 'Can you turn that music down, please?' Writing them out, they feel like nothing. Living them is the most conspicuous thing I have ever done.

The day my daughter is immunised – four now, and no longer a baby at all – she scrunches her face and shuts her eyes tight. Her hands squeeze mine as firmly as any adult grip. I sense her leave. 'So quiet,' the nurse comments. 'So well-behaved.' It feels like the start of something I can't quite grasp and definitely don't like: the complimenting of female compliance. 'Thank you for not burdening us with your cries.' It is okay that she doesn't, I want her to be exactly how she is, but I console her as though she does, because I know the pain is the same. It must be.

When she opens her eyes, she is surprised to find herself still in the doctor's office. We talk about where I go when I'm in pain and whether she might do the same. I hope she understands, and feels understood. I talk for far too long and she changes the subject to Freddo frogs. I did promise. While she eats the head off the smiling amphibian, I vow to always bear witness to her pain. Or, if she'd rather, she can take it somewhere private while I look after the body left where she stands: her eyes, her mouth, her skin, the feet in her shoes.

A shorter version of this essay was originally published by SBS Voices – © *SBS.*

WRITERS ON LOVE
AND AUTISM

There was a tweet going around last year about the 'five neurodivergent love languages' that has remained stuck in my head ever since.

Myth Schaber
@neurowonderful
The five neurodivergent love languages: infodumping, parallel play, support swapping, Please Crush My Soul Back Into My Body, and 'I found this cool rock/button/leaf/etc and thought you would like it'

It was written as what I imagine to be a playful and light-hearted take on *The Five Love Languages*, a 1990s relationship advice book by Gary Chapman. Since a quick google has revealed Chapman to have some not-great views, I am taking these neurodivergent love languages as the only ones I will pay attention to moving forward. The list demonstrates both how so much of the dialogue around love is neurotypical-specific, and the ways that neurodivergent people are subverting this by writing themselves into the discourse. So often something that an autistic person throws out onto social media in this kind of casual way will hit the nail on the head of an autistic experience far better than any diagnostic criteria ever can.

Info-dumping, as the term suggests, is the sharing of a great deal of information in one go. For autistic people, learning about specialist interests can be a passion, and sharing that acquired knowledge is an act of love. *Parallel play* is a term often used for children, but as an adult I like to think of it as being alone, together. Being in the company of someone, while doing my own thing. *Support swapping* is being aware of other people's support needs, and helping to manage them. Like when my neurodivergent friends text our group chat to remind each other to drink water. *Please Crush My Soul Back Into My Body* is about deep pressure input for stress management, and *'I found this cool rock'* is a form of gift-giving. It has also been called pebbling, after a penguin courtship ritual in which a male penguin will find the smoothest pebble to give to a female as a gift. If she likes it, she will place it in the nest and the pair will continue building up their pebble mound in preparation for the eggs.

Reaching out to other autistic authors, particularly those who write about love, has given me the opportunity to expand on this a little further. If you type 'romance writer' and 'autism' into a search engine, chances are the first name that is going to pop up is

Helen Hoang. Helen is the *New York Times* bestselling author of *The Kiss Quotient*, *The Bride Test* and *The Heart Principle*. Helen writes about love and autism because, being an autistic woman who loves romance novels, it is a natural fit.

'I didn't realize it when I wrote my first autistic romance [*The Kiss Quotient*], but I'd been craving love stories that explored the same challenges that I experience, such as difficulties with socializing, sensory issues, intimacy, mental health, and family dynamics,' she says. 'Hopefully this new genre of books can serve as a mirror for other autistic people and a window for those who wish to understand.'

US-based Australian author Jen Wilde echoes the sentiment. As the author of one of my favourite romantic coming-of-age novels, *Queens Of Geek*, it is no surprise to learn that Jen is a romantic at heart.

'Love is as natural to me as being autistic,' she says.

After going through primary school in unrequited love with a boy in her class, Jen says their high school years were punctuated with a stream of romantic pop culture across all mediums.

'My teen years were filled with romantic comedies that I watched over and over again, pawing through *Girlfriend* and *Dolly* magazines for tips on how to get my latest crush to notice me, and dreaming about the day I'd fall in love for real,' she says.

'I was obsessed with the idea of falling in love, I wanted romance and a Prince Charming to sweep me off my feet. I wanted that movie moment, when a heartthrob guy would spot me from across a crowded room and bam, my love story would begin.'

It is such a familiar longing, and the flipside to all that yearning for love is the feeling of not being worth much without it.

'I thought finding a boyfriend to love me would somehow prove to the world, and to myself, that I wasn't as broken as I felt,' Jen says. 'If I could get someone to love me, then surely I was normal, and all the kids who bullied me were wrong. I tried to fill my own insecurities with outside validation, and heal my traumas with relationships.'

The path to self-discovery is a long and bumpy one, as it is for so many autistic people.

'It would take years for me to find out I'm autistic, and even longer to figure out I'm queer, so while I knew I was different, I couldn't figure out why. I'd internalized from our heteronormative society [and all those romantic comedies and teen magazines] that the solution to my "brokenness" was hetero love. And when that didn't work, it only made me feel worse about myself.

'Once I discovered I'm autistic, and queer, everything started to change for me. I finally felt like I was living life on my terms. I'd spent so long mimicking and trying to fit in that I'd masked my own queerness even to myself, and letting that go was the beginning of my freedom.'

Jen writes beautiful novels for young adult (YA) readers, in part as a gift for their younger self.

'I write to show her that love is many incredible things, but it isn't the answer to trauma. And I write to show her that she isn't broken, she never was – it's the world that needs fixing.'

Australian YA author Anna Whateley tells me she loves to see the relationships develop between her characters in a way that feels authentic and real.

'Once the spark is there between two people I love being in the world they create together.'

Her novel *Peta Lyre's Rating Normal* is a stunning exploration of the many ways neurodivergent people are told and trained to be more 'normal', and what impact that can have on someone's relationships and sense of self.

Anna says she does not know if she could write non-autistic characters from a first-person perspective, as being autistic means looking at the world in that way.

'I'm autistic, so I naturally write with that window through which to look at the world. I can't know what it's like not to be neurodivergent,' she says.

'Physical disabilities are easier to leave out. That's precisely why I'm deliberately writing that part of me back in. I want our culture's literature to represent us, who we really are, and that includes ND/disabled folk. We all deserve a sense of belonging.'

•

When I read about love as written by an autistic writer, I do not feel as though I am doing it wrong. It no longer feels as though there is a 'right' way to do things, with every other way being 'wrong'. These conversations, and books, and tweets, have shifted my thinking towards something more self-affirming. That is the power of representation – maybe it is not important to everyone, but to some people it can mean the world.

PART FIVE

WHO I'M MEANT TO BE

I don't want my thoughts to die with me, I want to have done something. I'm not interested in power, or piles of money. I want to leave something behind. I want to make a positive contribution – to know that my life has meaning.

Temple Grandin, autistic writer and advocate

NOOR (1)

Noor relishes her role as an aunty to her little nephew, babysitting any chance she can get. She likes to get on his level, engage with him in all kinds of play, and see the world through the eyes of a child. The time spent caring for a little one in her own gentle way helps her to realise that parenthood does not mean she has to do things how they were done in her household when she was growing up. She does not need to be an authoritarian parent, or someone who looms over their child, invoking feelings of fear and unease. Noor and her husband know deep down they want to have a family of their own, to create a household full of unconditional love and acceptance. When Noor falls pregnant about two years into their marriage, the couple is delighted. It is a beautiful time in both their lives.

'I am so grateful I had a fun pregnancy. I was happy, I didn't have my periods to worry about. I had happy hormones, all that kind of stuff,' she says. 'It was really nice, except for the haemorrhoids. And I learned pretty quickly it wasn't socially acceptable to talk about haemorrhoids.'

It is the post-partum period she finds difficult. As her body is healing and her hormones are changing, sleep deprivation makes everything harder.

'Those early baby days were incredibly beautiful and incredibly stressful,' she says.

Noor feels in tune with her daughter from very early on.

'She was always very intense. I just accepted that was what she was like. I hadn't had any babies, so I had nothing to compare the experience to. It was really tiring; the sleep was just not happening. She would wake constantly, feed constantly. I was completely shattered, all the time.'

Noor is thankful her mother is around to help, and her husband is hands-on as well.

'Mum made sure there was always food I could eat, she was doing everything seamlessly in the background.'

Her husband, meanwhile, works, buys groceries, gives Noor back rubs to help with her pain and holds their daughter when she isn't feeding so Noor can rest. They don't let many people into their home during this time, as people are very forthcoming with their opinions on the ways a baby 'should' behave – and, in the case of Noor's daughter, sleep.

'Whatever magical baby could just be put down and be fine with it, that was not our baby.'

Noor and her husband take it in turns to hold her while bouncing on a Swiss ball to get her to sleep. She will only sleep in their arms. It seems as though just about anything will wake her.

'My poor daughter had such a hard time. I'm really grateful I was always inclined towards gentle parenting anyway. I might have tried sleep training for like three minutes and I gave up. It felt inhumane. It went against every fibre of my being. And lo and behold the science comes out saying you're not supposed to make your child dissociate from stress, and they have high cortisol in that state, so I feel positive about my choices. But it's tough, man.'

The early days of new parenthood are testing in ways only new parents can fully grasp. Noor sees her therapist to help her work through the challenges: the lack of alone time; the anxiety; the physical changes; and striking a balance between supporting her own needs and meeting those of a baby entirely dependent on her for food, comfort and regulation. Her psychiatrist tells her she needs to prioritise sleep for her mental health, and although it is sound advice, it is hard to implement with a high-needs child to care for.

'We got through it. I honestly don't know how we did. You just do. It helped that I didn't have to go back to work right away, so I recognise the privilege in that.'

Noor does go back to teaching part-time when her daughter is ten months old, and finds the time away from parenting to be good breathing space.

As Noor's daughter grows older, from baby to toddler, Noor sees that her sensitivities are not 'going away'; she does not need Noor less, as people assure you will happen when you are deep in those early days. It is quite the opposite, actually.

'I could see that the reason why she needs me so much more is because the world is just so intense for her, and I am her safe space,' Noor says.

When their daughter is nearly three, they welcome a second daughter into the family. She is the polar opposite of their first baby; she sleeps and does not mind being put in her crib. The contrast is a further marker of Noor's oldest daughter's needs, and they start to seek some more support for her.

The first diagnosis they get for her is sensory processing disorder (SPD). While SPD is not included in the *DSM-5*, it is a fairly well-known diagnosis, often given by occupational therapists for children who are overwhelmed by sensory information, seek out sensory experiences or avoid certain experiences. According to other professionals, including some psychologists and paediatricians, sensory issues are related to broader conditions, like autism and ADHD. It is a tricky space to navigate as a parent just looking for ways to support your child, especially when they are clearly struggling. The need to wade into these waters quickly, and to know how to see past the ableist, harmful framework to find affirming and supportive ways to help them is intense.

Noor starts taking her daughter to occupational therapy and play therapy, both of which seem to be positive experiences, but they do not seem to be enough. There is an anxiety-driven rigidity to her daughter.

'Something else was going on,' Noor says. 'I knew my daughter is different, and that I'm different.'

When her daughter is diagnosed as autistic, Noor begins her deep dive into educating herself about what that means. She sees herself in what she reads, and comes to understand herself as autistic. Being autistic herself, though, means that a lot of autism parenting spaces don't feel welcoming to her, with their emphasis on the tragedy of having an autistic child.

'I realised I needed to stay away from autism mum blogs,' she says. 'I found them so unhelpful and demeaning.'

Autistic advocate Kristy Forbes talks about the parenting journey that starts with parents being indoctrinated into viewing autism as a tragedy and a hardship to be overcome.

'It is horrendous,' she says. 'It is what broke our family, to be honest. [H]ere I was with these beautiful children, and I was initiated into this system.'

Kristy says it is not early intervention itself that is the issue, but the cover-all approach itself that does not take individual support needs into account – whether a child needs certain therapies, like speech pathology, occupational therapy and psychology – and often aims to make a child 'less autistic'.

'They are not even about increasing or accentuating the wonderful parts of who our children are. It is not about improving a person's quality of life; it's about adapting them. It is about having them be compliant, it is about having them look like a neurotypical kid.'

And when this kind of approach is suggested straight after a diagnosis, it can feel like a lot of pressure on families who are already adjusting to this new information.

'This heightens the anxiety of families, because they are also told there is a small window of opportunity between zero to five where their child can adapt their behaviour to look "normal". The first five years of a child's life, as we know in child development, are the most important foundational years [for] connecting with the people around them, forming bonds with the people who love them, but as soon as the word autism is also applied to that child, we forget all of that and go: "Okay, it's a race against time to normalise this child, it's not okay for them to be autistic." And then as parents we project into the future. Oh my god, will they make it at school? Will they be okay? Will people understand them? We spend the first few years explaining our children to everybody, qualifying their behaviour, justifying the way they are to the world, and you also have professionals telling you who your child is, telling you what is best for your children. And though you might have an intuition about what is good and right for your child, you kind of ignore that, and the thread that connects you directly to your child is slowly frayed until you are completely disconnected from your child, from your partner, from yourself, from your other children.'

Kristy is speaking from firsthand experience about the impact that this approach has had on her family.

'All of your focus is on your child not being autistic, and it is horrible. So families are beginning below a baseline and coming into the autistic community, where there is a risk they will be treated really poorly because they don't use language that is maybe identity-first, or inclusive. As parents, we haven't been exposed to positive autistic identity, we are coming from a medical model, a system where we have been disconnected and disempowered. So there has to be a space for families to enter, where somebody can put out their hand and say, "You know what? I know. I know. And it's going to be okay now." Because those people have been battered by the system and they need somebody who can love and nurture them as families.'

Autistic-led support groups and agencies with a focus on an affirming approach are starting to fill this void, but there is a lot of work to be done for families to learn that their way of doing things, in support of one or more autistic family members, is not dysfunctional.

'It takes years to convince families that it's okay if your child doesn't eat at the table, that it's okay if your child makes the noises they do to express joy, because the first years of that child's life and those families being immersed in that system has done so much damage to them,' Kristy says. 'I was that parent, we were that family. I remember this one day when I thought, "Okay, I can't go on like this. I want to be happy. I am ready to be happy." I thought, "I am going to find communities . . ." I couldn't find a single one. Every time I thought that I found a forum or a group, I'd get in there, and I would be there for half an hour at best, and it was just doom and gloom, and it was trauma, and it was projecting into the future and forgetting who our children are now and enjoying them. I don't begrudge those families, I get it, I understand it 100 per cent. There are so many of us who don't have the luxury of leaving our homes to be with other people, there are so many people who are at crisis point, who are living with a lot of shame because they can't keep up with the housework, because they have got their own chronic illnesses, or because there is other stuff going on.'

With InTune Pathways Kristy has built the kind of online community she herself was looking for, with virtual education and longer programs for families.

Finding her way to self-advocacy groups, as well as a coaching session with Kristy Forbes, is a game-changer for Noor.

'I learned [undiagnosed autism] is really common for mums and daughters,' she says. 'I learned about how to frame the language, so it isn't deficit-based. I could literally feel myself exhale with relief that I wasn't doing it wrong.'

It is huge, and Noor feels fortunate to have her husband's support through it all.

'I have probably been masking my whole life. The only person who has really seen me is my husband, he gets the full impact of everything. And he holds space for me. I feel safe in that anchoring connection with him, that he loves and accepts me for exactly who I am.'

As parents with autistic children will know, diagnosis is only one step, and accessing the right kind of support is an ongoing process. Her mother-in-law, who has an 'old school' approach to parenting, is insistent that their daughter needs a firmer hand.

'She said we just needed to discipline her, there needed to be consequences, and punishment.'

Noor says her journey with her daughter reflects her own self-acceptance.

'It's always the deficit model first, right? It's always behavioural therapy. And that didn't sit right with me. It didn't feel right. I wouldn't want to be rewarded with a star if I have a shower. I had to stop one particular therapist from coming to the house because it wasn't going well. My daughter was crying, she was miserable, and I just thought, "What is this? This can't be right."'

Noor now screens therapists before they meet her daughter. She researches, and makes it clear she does not view being autistic as a deficit – it is simply a different neurotype.

'I want her to be supported and accepted and celebrated. And once I feel intuitively as a mum that the therapist gets it, great, we can proceed,' she says.

Noor goes with her, stays with her, and it is a slow, gradual release as her daughter grows to trust a new therapist. Interruptions to routine like illness or lockdown make this harder, but Noor's view on this is something I wish to take away as a lesson for myself: 'It's inherently a way of teaching my daughter that things change, people change, but I'm always there.'

Balancing her own needs with her daughter's is an ongoing exercise, which is affected by what stage of her menstrual cycle Noor is at, and what else is going on in their lives.

'There are always challenges. Like, we just got back from a holiday, and my daughter was anxious on the day we travelled, and anxious on the day we left, so she only truly settled in the middle. That anxiety translated to whininess, rigidity, distress – so basically not a very fun holiday experience, even though she really wanted to go to the beach.'

Travelling as an autistic parent with an autistic child is a particular kind of stress, and one that takes a bit of time to come down from afterwards. There are so many more things to consider than non-autistic people seem to worry over, from whether accommodation is going to have proper blackout blinds, to whether there is going to be access to familiar foods and enough space in the itinerary for sufficient downtime.

Noor is still recovering from her holiday.

'If I am well rested, if I am Zen, if I am calm enough, I can hold space for her. But when I am out of my comfort zone as well, when I'm also travelling and I'm not in my routine, it is much harder to be calm.'

When I ask Noor what a typical family day is like, she laughs. Do I mean a high-energy day or a low-energy day? It is a differentiation I completely understand. Sometimes, as an autistic parent, it can be a challenge just to get out the door.

A high-energy day is one spent at the playground or the park. It is an outdoorsy, fun kind of day – but then there's the other kind: 'It's sensory overload to go out, for all of us. If it's sweaty and hot, I'm sticky, the kids are sticky. If we need to get them to the toilet quickly, oh no, they don't want that toilet, it's too wet and stinky. I get it, I don't like random stinky toilets either.'

A low-energy day is better spent at home watching movies, eating popcorn, or having a picnic lunch in the garden. Noor admits those are the days she prefers.

'Home feels safe. That's what I like about being home with my kids. Being on our screens. We aren't turning into zombies; we are spending time together.'

We talk about screen time, and how our attitudes towards it has changed with a growing understanding of being neurodivergent, and of parenting neurodivergent kids. Noor says her husband is still triggered by it, having been raised with the attitude that 'screen time is bad'.

'He's working on it, he's realising how good it is, how it helps us regulate. It's a nice break when everything else is so overwhelming.'

The calmness of home is a contrast to the busyness of large family events. Noor's husband has a big family that spends a lot of time together.

'Those early years I really had to learn a lot of rules, so many rules to do with his family and how things are done. That was a big chunk missing from my childhood, as we were really isolated. So imagine marrying into this massive, well-functioning family. It was a lot to take in at the beginning. Ten years on I have pretty much got the hang of it. I still don't like big gatherings. I still don't like surprise visits, and I still don't like late nights.'

These days Noor manages this by setting boundaries around what she can and can't do, and her youngest daughter often goes with her father to events that she herself does not feel up for.

'We've worked out a system that is doing well for the most part,' she says. 'Now I know it's okay not to like [large gatherings]. I can just go for a little while, it's okay to leave early. It's okay to accept that this is how I'll always be. I'm never going to be one to volunteer to host a big do. That's just not me.'

Noor makes the important point that in learning to advocate for herself and set boundaries around what she is and isn't able to do, she is showing her oldest daughter how to do that as well. And part of that is knowing that some people will not get it.

'Sometimes I say to my daughter, "Okay, this person doesn't understand your brain. She means well, she just doesn't understand your brain. Not the way we do."'

When I ask her what she hopes to teach her daughter about being autistic, Noor replies: 'I will definitely say to her that it's the way Allah created you and me. And there's nothing ever wrong in that. Even if the wider world or people who are not very kind say that [it is], don't ever believe it. I will tell her: I'm your biggest ally, and you're perfect as you are. Basically, all the things I wish I had heard from my parents when I was growing up. I don't want her to link her worth to her output. It's great to have a work ethic; it's not great to kill yourself over it. It's important to know when to rest. I want to teach her to be self-aware, to reach out for help when she needs it.'

TIM

'I don't respond when you talk. I flap my arms, make noise, and may even lie on the floor. This is what you see. Severe autism. Severe autism means I can only process one thing at a time, so I have to work hard to understand things. I am also hypersensitive and everyday sensations can be painfully intense. With both of these difficulties, I am constantly anxious and overwhelmed. When I was a toddler, I was way behind in my development. I didn't turn my head when others called me. I didn't speak. I didn't respond to people. I played with toys by lining them up and spinning anything that turns. When I got overwhelmed, I would lie on the floor, eyes shut, hands on my ears, and be totally in my own world. My mum saw the unseen, the potential to be fully human, to live a satisfying life.'

This is how Tim starts his TED Talk, which is then uploaded and made accessible to the world online. When eighteen-year-old

Tim comes on stage at the Melbourne Recital Centre with his mum Sarah, you can hear a pin drop, as the audience is withholding their applause for sensory reasons. Tim uses his communication device to talk about his experiences learning to communicate and the path to inclusive education. It is a challenge that at first seems overwhelming for Tim. Fresh from a high school experience that left him feeling isolated for being different, appearing in front of a large audience to talk about his traumatic experiences is a daunting prospect. But recognising that this is a golden opportunity to advocate for those who do not have access to a voice, he accepts the invitation.

He works on the draft for his speech with his mum, his sister and I CAN Network CEO and friend Chris Varney. It is Chris, whose autistic-led organisation runs group-mentoring programs with autistic young people around the country, promoting a respectful, strengths-based view of autism, who initially asks Tim if he would like to present at the TEDxMelbourne event. Chris had studied law with Tim's sister. She thought Tim would get something out of Chris's I CAN work, so Chris and Tim arranged to meet for coffee.

Chris recalls: 'We met in this cafe. Tim sat down and said, "I believe I could mentor and be mentored." I was so impressed by him. I could see that he was doing a lot of work to regulate and manage huge hypersensitivities. Tim and Sarah really taught me a lot about the non-speaking autistic experience.'

Chris calls the lead-up to and execution of the TED Talk a marathon, and it is one that Tim commits to wholeheartedly. He revises his speech – the theme of which is 'Seeing the Unseen' – more than ten times, and with the help of those around him he is able to envision himself going through each step of the process, from arriving at the venue to stepping up on to the stage.

'Tim was truly epic,' Chris says. 'It is not often people are immersed in a message like this, and Tim was hitting them between the eyes with his perspective and experiences.'

Tim finds the experience both overwhelming and incredibly gratifying. The success of his talk helps him to regain some of his confidence in himself, and to see a way forward doing meaningful work.

Chris says Tim's drive is incredible to see in action. 'Tim pushes himself. He is ambitious, hardworking . . . Having non-speaking advocates is so important. Unfortunately people often put non-speaking autistics into the too-hard basket. That is why Tim's work is so important.'

Tim flags his past experiences with advocates in high school as the starting point for his own advocacy work. He wants to be able to support other autistic people in the ways he was supported.

'I got interested in advocacy when disability advocates came in to bat for me at high school. I became keen to learn self-advocacy by looking at how they work, their use of legislation and strategies for inclusion, and how they negotiate with schools for access and participation for students like me.'

Tim's voice is a powerful one, encapsulating the importance of 'nothing about us without us', a slogan used for disability activism that first came into use in the 1990s. Tim is constantly working to find new ways to advocate for non-speaking people, and continues his working relationship with Chris and the I CAN Network as an ambassador for the organisation. Due to high anxiety and sensory and movement issues, Tim is still working on becoming a mentor to other autistic non-speaking students.

'By good fortune, Chris asked me to give some presentations [for I CAN] and participate in working groups. More opportunities came along for presentations, which I've been able to learn from to be better at putting my message across,' he says.

•

In *We're Not Broken: Changing the Autism Conversation*, autistic journalist and author Eric Garcia discusses the history of autism advocacy, and how it has created a tension between parent advocacy and self-advocacy.

He writes: 'From the 1970s to the mid-2000s, much of the political advocacy for autism was done without the input of autistic people. The fact that autism existed on a spectrum and that autistic people could speak (either through their physical voices or via communication devices) and advocate for themselves was not widely known until the 1990s.'

Outlining the history of advocacy, he observes that 'the early era of autism advocacy in the 1970s was meant as an act of taking back power for parents who had been blamed for their children's autism for years . . . and as a result of parent advocates dominating the conversation, autistic people themselves wound up missing out on much of the disability rights movement that animated the twentieth century.'

Garcia's book is a must-read, and I keep coming back to this point he made about advocacy: 'The problem with focusing on the parents of autistic people instead of the autistic people themselves is that when these two sides clash, society tends to sympathise with parents.'

This historical context is not intended to paint all parents of autistic people as driven by unrealistic expectations or defeatism in the face of insurmountable difficulties, with resulting poor parenting. In my experience, most are actually incredible. And as Kristy Forbes points out, society sets us up to view autism as a negative. We are constantly reminded of all of the things our children will not be able to do. And yet so many parents are going up against systems – systems that often chewed us up and spat us out as children, or systems we were taught to revere – and we are fighting for our children to get support and a fair go. Parents are often painted as overly anxious, or too precious, or lacking in the skills to adequately discipline our children. This is a prevalent misconception to do with a lack of understanding of the immensely challenging job of parenting neurodivergent children. In prioritising Tim's differences in the intake and processing of information, Sarah's work in advocating for and supporting Tim through his life, including those times when he himself was not able to self-advocate, speaks to this kind of strength of character. It is not an easy role, not when people still meet the disclosure 'my child is autistic' with 'I am so sorry'. But parents keep advocating in the hope that attitudes will change, that their children – and all autistic children – will have equality, understanding, kindness and acceptance from their communities, with opportunities to participate more fully in society throughout their lives.

•

In his own advocacy, Tim has also been involved in organisations such as Communications Rights Australia, Youth Disability Advocacy Services, Children and Young People with Disability Australia and Reframing Autism. His work in these spaces is making a mark, and he is turning his struggles and pain into better outcomes for those who come after him.

'I believe that advocacy for people without speech, one of the most marginalised groups, is essential for access and participation and to have a voice. Therefore, I hope to learn more about how to advocate effectively to bring socially just outcomes.'

The most rewarding experiences of Tim's advocacy work include the feedback from families with autistic children who reach out to him for ideas on supporting their children, or to let him know how his story resonates with theirs. Both Tim and Sarah are gratified and touched by the courage, resilience and motivation of these families to keep advocating for their children and other autistic people.

CHLOË

Chloë has long known she has a strong sense of social justice, and university is where she finds somewhere to direct all that energy and passion. As a multiply-disabled autistic woman, she has skin in the game.

'I got really into student advocacy because I can't let something go if it's wrong. I have to fix it, until I have exhausted all channels,' she says.

Her skills and expertise in this area see her taking a role on the university's Academic Board for two years as an undergraduate representative.

'One of those years was the first year of the pandemic, so I spent a lot of time advocating for compassionate grading policies and really fighting for those,' she says.

Once these policies are in place, Chloë continues to fight for these to be retrospectively added to students who had their exams at the start of the pandemic. It is a nightmare in terms of legalities, but she gets it done. Alongside that, she is in the disability and carers department in the student union.

'It just kind of happened and I realised I had a knack for it, for advocacy,' she says. 'I really like applying those skills to disability advocacy.'

Her work in this field sees her win the Vice-Chancellor's Excellence Award for diversity and inclusion, as well as a National Award for Disability Leadership, accolades that make her realise she should be proud of what she has achieved.

'I will [always continue to advocate], because I can't let an injustice go. It's good to have an outlet, doing proactive work like this, so I don't feel the need to advocate for every little thing in my life,' she says.

Kristy Forbes embraces advocacy and support work for a similar reason – she wants families to feel empowered.

'I want neurodivergent culture to be normalised, instead of constantly being compared to neuronormativity, and us being othered. Because we are not disordered, we do have our own identity and culture,' she says.

'There can't be millions of us all over the world who share so many aspects of our lives and our beings, and all of us just be disordered. I mean, there are some really wonderful things about our culture, and rather than expecting them to change, I think sometimes it is more helpful to work with the people, and the families, and to present them with reframes around things so they can forgive themselves, so they can feel a sense of relief, of self-compassion, of self-love, and start to do things a bit differently.

I think that is more powerful than anything. I think it is great that people are fighting the system. There are many families who don't have a choice about whether they are immersed in that system or not, too, so when we can empower them with a really positive understanding of themselves as families, that has a greater impact.'

•

Chloë is also on the Youth Council for a national disability organisation and works part-time for a non-profit autism organisation.

'It's so much fun to get to talk to autistic people and think of ways to bring autistic people in, and different stories I can tell, and finding someone to tell that story.'

Chloë sees this work as sitting comfortably alongside her future in engineering.

'Eventually I want to keep doing two different things, because I can't imagine doing the same thing nine to five. That sounds boring, and my job is so exciting. In engineering, when will I get to see all these things come to fruition, to meet all these people?'

In the workplace, Chloë sees her disabilities as part of her strengths and what she is able to bring to the table.

'In engineering, I want to be hired as a disabled engineer, not in spite of, not without acknowledging my disabilities, and to work with a company that is willing to invest in innovation in terms of accessibility, that sees it as part of sustainability and wants to spend the money there, rather than sticking to minimum standards.'

In Australia, there are building standards that must be adhered to under the *Disability Discrimination Act (1992)*. These are mostly to do with access to buildings, and facilities and services within buildings, with a focus on wheelchair access. They provide a base level of what is legally required, but Chloë envisions accessibility as being so much more than that.

'It could be the gold standard,' she says.

With all the energy she is devoting to these passions and this important work, Chloë is also thinking more about the power of rest.

'The pandemic was the first time I've understood masking. I've actually unmasked. I know this because when I went back [to uni and work], I noticed how much effort it takes. I truly understood it, because it was the longest respite I'd ever had,' she says.

Covid and Melbourne's many lockdowns force her to cut back, and to prioritise balance.

'Previously, I have managed to avoid burnout by neglecting areas of my life,' she says. 'My uni will go down the drain, or something else will slip. Now, rather than "I will do all of it to the end of me", self-preservation kicks in. I am acutely aware going into employment, I am cognisant of how likely burnout is. That's why I want to do two part-time jobs, because if I just do one job I will fill all my downtime with interesting things, fun things, advocacy, because I need more stimulation. And if I do that I will crash and burn, and probably lose the end of my twenties recovering from that.'

It is a level of self-awareness I wish I had had in that period of my life. Chloë says having a particular interest in learning how to manage her time and energy has helped.

'I am blessed with knowledge in that area. There were probably periods in high school where [burnout] happened. Depression phases I've had were probably linked more to burnout than anything else. My ADHD diagnosis helped because I developed better strategies.'

When she isn't working and advocating and spending time with her friends and partner, Chloë has a bit of time left for exploring her special interests, which have included plants, make-up, handmade earrings, crafting, stationery and bullet journalling.

'I've learnt that with ADHD, systems last for six months for me and then they are not fun anymore and that's fine. It's okay to change systems,' she says. 'The merit of the system is not for how long you do it; it's whether it is useful for you at that point in time.'

She distinguishes between special interests and hyperfocuses, saying she has more of the latter these days.

'I will crochet for two weeks nonstop. Productivity is another [interest], but in the sense of [working out the] best strategies for how to get the most out of my time, not how to be the best worker bee . . . I had strategies for ADHD before I knew I had it. For example, I made visual checklists where I would manually move something to "done" so I would get enough of a [dopamine] reward. Once I found out I had ADHD that all made sense.'

Chloë's interest and knowledge around productivity is infectious, and her advice has actually helped me enormously with completing this book by deadline.

'Work takes up a certain amount of time, so I want to be productive in my hours outside of that. And that includes getting enough rest, because that is productive too. So, I love learning about that, and helping other people with it too.'

Some of Chloë's tips that have helped me have included using a yearly wall planner, writing daily and weekly to-do lists, and scheduling downtime. On a more profound level, it is Chloë's observations on her own sensitivity that will stick with me. She speaks to the experience of harnessing her sensitivity for autistic joy. As a child it was dizzy-whizzies that gave her that feeling; as an adult it is often music.

'When [Australian indie band] Ball Park Music released the song "Cherub", the first time I listened to it I was paralysed with euphoria from the instrumental build. I honestly could not move until about the third time I listened to the song. I lay there on my bed, grinning, with tears forming. I listened to it on repeat throughout the morning (and indeed the rest of the day). I came downstairs and listened to it while making breakfast, and the sun was shining through the suncatcher crystal in the kitchen, so I just gazed at the rainbows and listened to the song on repeat,' she recalls.

She listens to the song more than a hundred times in two days – quite the feat given it is more than five minutes long. Chloë sees the band live as often as she can, and when she does she takes her noise-dulling earplugs out just for 'Cherub'.

'I let the overstimulation wash over me like a wave. It's not a bad overstimulation; it's a very good one. I sing my heart out, trying to absorb every second and burn it deep into my memory.'

Experiencing joy on a whole different sensory level is a part of being autistic Chloë likes a lot. I think of my daughter stim-dancing with her soft, floating feathers. I think of myself in the garden, watering lavender in the sun.

'Being very sensitive may mean things are hard, but it also means that I can experience good things in ways non-autistics can never even fathom,' Chloë says.

JESS

J ess and Jesslyn take a couple of deep breaths, and head into the convention hall. It is Jesslyn's idea, and one that Jess helps bring to life along with a group of friends they have made from playing *World of Warcraft* online. It is loud, and busy, and overwhelming, but it turns out to be one of the best weekends of their lives. The *My Little Pony* fandom is at its peak, and it is as though the writers of the cartoon television show have used Jesslyn as a model for the character of Fluttershy, the shy, kind, animal-loving Pegasus pony who is one of the six main characters.

'Fluttershy is literally Jesslyn,' says Jess. 'Every time she would do something on the show, we would say, "Oh my god, that's you!"

'We had a group of friends who had mostly come from playing *WoW* with us, or people who we had met online, and they wanted to dress up as *My Little Pony* characters with us, because Jesslyn wanted to cosplay Fluttershy but didn't want to do it on her own.'

Jess dresses up as Rainbow Dash, the impulsive and loyal Pegasus pony whom she sees a lot of herself in. Their friends take the other roles.

The *My Little Pony* fandom is considered part of the New Sincerity trend, which moves away from postmodern irony and cynicism. It is about celebrating the things one likes, and sharing that appreciation with others. *By the early 2010s, the show has found a large audience of adult fans and formed its own online subculture, with artwork, music, and writing shared on sites like Tumblr, Twitter and Reddit, as well as dedicated fan sites.* As someone who grew up in a time when it was uncool to care about pretty much anything, this sounds so much more appealing.

Jess is initially worried about how the day is going to go, because she has seen a lot of cruelty directed towards plus-size cosplayers online, but it turns out to be a day of unbridled joy.

'We have never had so much positive attention and excitement for a cosplay in our lives,' she says. 'We could not walk two steps without someone stopping us and wanting a picture. The entire weekend, it was the most amazing thing that has ever happened. We rode on that high, it was so great.'

Jess starts to feel more comfortable in herself because of it, and the huge positive reaction gives her confidence to do it again. They go as ponies to several more conventions, sometimes with friends as the other ponies, and sometimes just the two of them as a couple. The experience sparks a love of cosplay and fandom conventions for the couple. Jess describes what those events are like as an autistic person.

'I was basically super-masking the whole time at a convention, because I was in character, so I would get home and crash,' she says. 'I would fall asleep and then after the Sunday, it would take a week to recover. I was *on* the whole time there. I was very aware of that at the time. And it was worth it.'

Jess says the trick is choosing a character whose persona is fun to be in for a length of time.

'I cosplayed Janet from *The Good Place* at the very last convention I went to before the pandemic. It was lovely to be Janet for a day: you walk around with a pleasant smile on your face the whole time, because you are in character. Janet is a joy to cosplay. So is Mabel Pines [from the Disney animation *Gravity Falls*] for that matter. Mabel is glitter and sunshine and excitement, and when you are putting that on for the whole weekend, it is not a negative drain; it *is* an energy drain, but it's not coming from a negative place. It is just really nice. It is nice getting to be that kind of person for a while.'

There are so many highlights, including making new friends and meeting actors and creators from their favourite shows. For Jess, cosplaying has been a big part of her de-masking journey, as has exploring other creative interests and pursuits more linked to her childhood.

'I tried figure-skating. I was rollerblading for a while, because I'd loved that as a kid, but all the rinks were a forty-minute drive from me. So I swapped to figure-skating on ice because the rink was closer. And I started ballet lessons again.

261

'I was really finding myself. I really like moving to music, I like this feeling of engaging everything in my body. There have been several years of finding myself in that way, and I am still finding new things I like.'

Jess shares a lot of autistic and ADHD memes and content on her Instagram page, and this has helped other people identify their own neurodivergence for the first time.

'I saw that stuff on Tumblr back in the day. When it's somebody talking about it from the inside, instead of cold, clinical, diagnostic language . . . it's no wonder I looked at my initial diagnosis and thought that can't be me, because it was all looking from the outside, not exploring how when X happens you react like Y because of Z,' she says. 'So yeah, sharing and connecting with community has been really good.'

The pandemic has been challenging for Jess, not least because she is considered an essential worker and has been working harder than ever throughout. It has also meant that conventions, as well as figure-skating and ballet, do not feel accessible anymore, both because of the crowds and because of the attitudes of people who seem to believe that the pandemic is over.

'I don't feel comfortable cosplaying at the moment, because of the thing when someone is dressed the same, or a fan of what you're dressed as, people will run up and want to give you a hug and I just do not have the mental space to deal with that right now. I don't have the mental space to be wearing a wig and a full face of make-up, and then a mask. I don't think I could cope with that, it's all too much.'

Jess and I talk about how we, as well as the other neurodivergent people in our lives, seem to be having a particularly difficult time these past few years. Research shows that while the COVID-19 pandemic has had a negative psychological and mental health impact on all people, this impact is likely to be stronger for autistic people. For me, it is the mental bandwidth being used to process such large-scale grief and loss, combined with the whiplash of witnessing people willingly spread a virus when they do not know how it will impact other people. Jess shares similar sentiments.

'We've been in danger mode for over three years now. We've been constantly on, heightened, and we've got nothing left. Even neurotypical people are struggling,' she says.

Animals continue to bring Jess a lot of joy, though, and you would be hard-pressed to find better pet parents than her and Jesslyn. The couple stopped getting rats after a couple of years because of their short lives and the respiratory conditions they develop in pet shops (back when regulations were not really a thing), and they got a second cat, Bella the ragdoll. Ragdolls have a reputation for being cuddly and passive, but passive is not how Jess would describe Bella.

'She was a very naughty cat who wanted to explore all the forbidden places in the house, like behind the TV, and chew wires,' Jess says.

They eventually lost their first cat, Lenore, to lymphoma in 2017 and Bella to advanced kidney disease in 2019, having given them long and beautiful lives. The heartbreak of losing an animal is the price we pay for all of the love they bring into our lives, as I know well from the loss of our family dog, Mack.

Jess remembers each pet for their unique traits and personalities, even those long gone. Along with beautiful Bunford, they had another bunny called Wiggles, bought from a pet shop.

'This was before we were educated about backyard breeders and the high rate of dumping once they stop being small and cute and willing to be cuddled. We only adopt now,' she says.

'Over the years we had a lot of health scares with Wiggles. We spent so much money on the emergency vet but we would have done anything to help her.'

After losing Wiggles at age four, they adopted a new friend for Bunford, Ladybun, who was sunshine and happiness in bunny form. They were together for three years, until Ladybun became very sick.

'It was devastating to lose her,' Jess says.

Pepper, a very shy bunny, was adopted next. Bunford and Pepper made great friends. Then in early 2020, during lockdown, Jesslyn noticed a lump on Bunford's back. They took him to the vet and found out it was cancer.

'He was already slowing down a lot with his arthritis and cataracts, but as the cancer grew he struggled to hop around and keep his balance. We were giving him meds every twelve hours, cleaning his underside because he could no longer do it himself, rolling up towels in the cage so he could prop himself up. You could see the determination burning away, he wasn't ready to go. Then one day, he kept licking and licking Jesslyn. Whenever we took him into the bedroom for a cuddle, the licking meant "I'm done now, please take me to the cage". He was communicating that he wanted to go.

'Our vet friend came over and put Bunford to sleep so we wouldn't have to drive him to the local clinic and risk one of us being unable to be in the room with him due to lockdown restrictions. He also hated the car and the vet clinic so this was one final thing we could do for him. It was awful. We're both still not over losing him and it's been more than two years.'

It's clear that Bunford was a healing presence, a very special animal. After the devastation of his death, their other bunny Pepper got quite lonely, and Jess and Jesslyn started looking to adopt again.

'The same vet friend came through with a bunny family. We fostered to adopt the boys, with their mum and siblings, they were only six weeks old and needed to be with mum for another two weeks. That gave us plenty of time to learn all of their person-alities and choose which ones would get along with Pepper the best. So we have three bunnies now,' she says.

Currently the couple has the fluffy black cat Toothless, ragdoll Floof, and Pepper, Smudge and Noodle the bunnies. They are all very loved and spoiled.

'Having pets has brought me so much joy and comfort. Being able to cuddle and pat them – when they allow it – and having a cat lying on my chest purring at me is so soothing,' Jess says.

Right now, Jess is also finding joy in making things like buttons out of resin, and in spinning yarn and knitting. She has been knitting on and off since she was a child; it was something she used to do with her nan.

Jess's relationship with her family is much closer these days, and Jess says her perspective has changed a lot in recent times. She can see now that her mum never stopped fighting for her.

'For Mother's Day one year I wrote her a long card saying pretty much all that, that it wasn't her fault and that I was sorry I had been so distant and angry about it for so many years. We both cried.'

Jess and her mum have also bonded over Jess's crafting hobbies.

'Sometimes I'll call and we'll chat on the phone for over an hour about [knitting and crafting and sewing], or we will meet up at the local yarn store and go shopping, then have lunch somewhere.'

Exploring these hobbies means her gaming is balanced with other pursuits.

'I still do it, but it's no longer in an obsessive "must block out the world" way,' she says. 'It's much healthier now.'

She is doing her best to get through each day, to spend time with Jesslyn, to visit the birds near her house, to keep being creative, to look after herself and find moments of joy with her animals. And that is enough.

MICHAEL

The months after Michael's appearance on *Love on the Spectrum* see his social media and inbox flooded with messages of support from fans of the show. He describes the impact this has on his self-esteem and feelings of self-worth.

'In high school, my self-confidence was low. It has built up at a very slow pace. I still felt inferior to a lot of people, but after appearing on *Love on the Spectrum* it started to build more quickly, especially after receiving all those messages,' he says. 'It made me realise that if these people can see the best in me, maybe I should too.'

Since the show, Michael has signed with a talent agent, launched a podcast (*Mr A+*) and started focusing more heavily on pursuing his acting dreams.

'I have kind of come to love the attention,' he says. 'Don't get me wrong – I don't go out looking for attention! Everything I'm doing – interviews, and my podcast and other opportunities – it's all leading to a brighter future; brighter than I could have imagined.'

When we talk about what he likes most about acting, Michael says it is what he can give to other people.

'Giving someone else joy gives me joy in return. To give an audience joy and laughter is a really rewarding experience.'

We talk about the industry he is in, and whether facing rejection as part of his pursuit is ever difficult. Michael says he is confident in auditions.

'Even if you don't get accepted for a role, it's not necessarily a bad thing because maybe that's just not the role for you. Because being told "no, you're not right for the role", that is just a setback, it's part of it.'

Part of this step towards his goals for the future is leaving behind a job he has worked at for the past five years in a kitchen-manufacturing company.

'I am so grateful for the job, but now is the time,' he says.

Michael has a few acting gigs lined up, and will be appearing on screens again soon.

'My goal has never been to be the greatest actor of all time; my plan has always been to become another addition to the long list of amazing actors. Acting is one of my top three passions, it's one of the three things I live for.'

The other two? Railways and animals. Michael is always ready to connect with other people over a shared love of these things.

'I've been a really avid fan of *Thomas the Tank Engine* for twenty-five years because I'm fascinated with the way trains work, especially steam locomotives.

'And animals are really amazing creatures; they are all very different. Some are quite distinctive, some are magnificent . . . The life of an animal is far more simple and a lot less complicated than that of a human. I admire that.'

These are special interests that have stayed with Michael throughout his life.

'If there is something I am passionate about, I could go on and on for hours about it,' he says. 'If I notice the other person is not interested, I will awkwardly change the subject to them, and what they might want to talk about.'

Michael's family are behind the scenes, celebrating every win with him. They are thrilled but not surprised to see how he is touching other people's lives. Michael is seeing now how right they were to have taught him to always be himself.

'If people can't accept you for who you are, that's their problem,' he says.

Michael also wants to help change people's perceptions of autism and what autistic people can achieve.

'I like to entertain and to bring love and light into people's lives. That's what I want to keep doing,' he says. 'We all want to be loved. We all want to connect with each other.'

And a little bird has told me that love might just be blossoming for Michael at this very moment . . .

NOOR (II)

When Noor's children are at school, or if they are home watching morning cartoons, she will always write. She schedules time for writing into her day – usually in the mornings, unless something else comes up.

'It's either me working on my book, or articles, or whatever else. Journalling, decompressing my own thoughts, it really helps,' she says.

'Because my brain is very project-based, I love chewing on problems, solving them. Life is ongoing, so it is good to have goals that are obtainable. I get that nice dopamine hit, and it helps when it's something I love to do.'

Noor also loves drawing, but regrets she has not had the chance to explore that part of herself because of her limited free time.

'I do hope to get to it more as my children get older,' she says. 'I would love to look into pottery, painting, more sensory things, but right now the easiest and quickest way to get anything down is on my laptop when my children are asleep at night or at school.'

Navigating culture and neurodivergence is a lifelong passion for Noor, and putting words to her experiences is incredibly important.

'It's really complicated as well. I'm not an out-and-proud autistic Muslim woman of colour. I'd like to be at some stage, when it's safer, because I don't ever want my daughter to feel ashamed of who she is, or who I am. At least within the walls of our home we can do that, but it's hard outside the home because, with things like going to gatherings, it's all in the design. When things are not designed with autistic children – and adults – in mind, it's not going to go well.'

Noor gives an example of this with an upcoming family wedding. It is going to be held at night, an 'absolute disaster', and she is annoyed by the expectation that she bring her children along and ensure they are well-behaved.

'You can't expect them to be on their best behaviour if they are tired and dysregulated,' she says.

Noor is thankful that she lives near mosques that are accommodating to women and children, but that is not the case everywhere.

'In many Muslim communities, women can't even get to mosques, let alone autistic women, let alone autistic children,' she says. 'I know the Muslim community has problems admitting to disability existing, let alone accommodating it. It's really sad, because through the Prophet Mohammed, peace be upon him, disability was already addressed in the Quran.'

Noor shares one of her favourite stories from the Quran, about how when a disabled man tried to ask the Prophet a question he frowned, and then a revelation from God came down to correct him.

'I mean, that's amazing. How do we translate that to real life, to my lived experience?' she ponders.

'It is uncomfortable for uncles at the mosque to be questioned on their privilege, like why aren't you making wheelchair ramps – it's a whole story, which can be confronting.'

These kinds of thoughts and discussions motivate Noor to keep writing and sharing her own experiences, her intersectional existence that she has not seen reflected in many other places.

'I wish there was more out there, because then we could see ourselves reflected in the myriad ways that we exist as human beings,' she says. 'And how there are so many odd quirks to us, [which are] expressed differently because of our different religions or backgrounds.'

Another way this manifests for Noor and her family is in the pressure to 'do Ramadan right'. In a piece she has written for *SBS Voices*, Noor outlines the difficulties she faces as an autistic parent during the month of fasting, prayer, reflection and community. It is particularly hard for her and her daughter to stay regulated when they are hungry.

Noor writes:

I want to model self-awareness and self-compassion for my daughters, especially my autistic daughter. There is a lot of pressure to 'do Ramadan right' but the baseline is always neurotypical and able-bodied, and doesn't take into account those of us who are disabled. It's harder for me to cope with hunger and thirst, it's harder for me to transition from task to task, and my demand-avoidance can make me too anxious to even do the things I enjoy.

My daughters watch me, imitate me, and I want to model values that can fortify their childhood and future selves. I want to keep talking to my daughters, especially my eldest, about privilege, and what actionable steps we can do to donate to others who are struggling, especially in this blessed month – not from a place of arrogance, but from a place of humility, service and compassion. Her deep sense of fairness would probably shape her into a social justice warrior one day. She is my very own Greta Thunberg.

I hope my daughters will look back at their childhood Ramadans as being a special month of reflection, stories, shared laughter, simple meals, interesting crafts – even if I get hangry every now and then.

For Noor, exploring these topics, of identity, culture, disability, family and belonging, both in her writing and in her life, is what it is all about.

'Showing up, being alive, teaching my daughter to love herself as she is, being patient with her, helping her to see she is already enough as she is and that she doesn't have to get into unhealthy relationships to feel loved, for her to recognise love in her family home so it's natural for that to flow on to choosing a life partner, as opposed to doing it the hard way, the way I did – that's what is important to me,' she says.

'For me, existing well and calmly is the ultimate act of resistance.'

•

Noor is getting better at prioritising couple time now that she is out of the woods of early parenthood, although sometimes it can be hard when she also needs time just for herself so she can decompress.

'Sometimes I just want to hide in the bedroom all night. My husband made a comment recently about how my laptop is my best friend, so I realised, yes, I've got to prioritise time with him too,' she says with a laugh.

When Noor talks about love in relation to her partner, I can see how this definition also encapsulates the way she parents her children.

'Love is safety. Love is acceptance. Love is being quietly held in all of your states and forms – the messy bits, the funny bits, the scary bits. And it is knowing that you can count on the safe person to be around to always catch you, no matter what, and that you don't have to bend yourself into all kinds of contorting shapes to be loved, to be who you are, and to be safe and seen.'

IN CONCLUSION

I have never been able to tell a succinct love story about me and my partner. There are too many moving parts, and I don't know how to figure out which ones are relevant. We met at a university bar, hardly a meet-cute, and we have been together for so many years that a monologue about our life together in chronological order would take too long. I could do it, if we had the time, but I am not sure anyone wants to listen to all of that. I could say, 'We have cycled through many iterations of ourselves, ebbing and flowing, and continuing to choose one another, every version along the way,' but that is a bit vague, isn't it? How about: 'There have been hard times, and many more good ones'? It sounds like it belongs on a greeting card, really.

Is it relevant that he met my Granda and entire family when he joined me in Ireland on Christmas Day, though we'd only known each other for a few weeks, and they all loved him immediately? Perhaps. Is it relevant that he went on the Giant Drop at Dreamworld with me on one of our first dates, disguising a fear of heights so intense that he still talks about this experience more than sixteen years later? Maybe not. Would it confuse matters if I said he was the email breakup I mentioned in that essay on running? Quite likely. I think it's probably, almost definitely relevant that he is the first person I have ever dated who did not try to 'educate' me on 'the right kind' of music, and instead came to watch bands I liked and danced like a goof, and that he changes his mind and adjusts his thinking when presented with new information, and knows how to listen and laugh and hold space and withhold judgement and meet people where they are at and show up for people and plant flowers and tell me when the moon looks pretty and prioritise kindness and and and . . .

You see? I'm no good at it. I get tangled in my thoughts and my words. Because a real, true thing is far trickier than a first kiss story, harder to pin down, and now that I think about it, I feel the same about being autistic. It would be easier to say that autism is X, Y and Z. A list of traits, a line from here to there. This could have been an operational manual: *The Guide To Being Autistic*™, subheading: *Or how to have an autistic person in your life*. But, of course, I would have done a terrible job of writing that, because autism is more than one thing or even a list of things. Luckily, in writing a whole book, I have not had to be succinct. Thoughts and threads have spread out over more than 250 pages. Every day and every year since learning this key piece of information about myself, understanding grows in my mind. If this was the Pixar movie *Inside Out*, autism would have its own little island in my mind. Whereas I used to think my propensity for sitting on the bed in a towel after a shower instead of immediately getting ready was laziness, now I understand about executive functioning. I can see that my need to switch the subtitles on whenever I watch something has less to do with audio quality and more to do with auditory processing. And this project has prompted so much new growth. That richness and range of experiences is what I have hoped to capture with these stories. Real lives are endlessly interesting in the uniqueness of the details and the commonality of the feelings.

In speaking to Michael, Jess, Noor, Tim and Chloë, I have been reminded over and over again that there is no blueprint for successful love or a successful life. There are countless ways to do this, and it is so much more about how it feels than how it looks. But as I interviewed each of them, I could not help but marvel at all the ways in which they love and are loved. And I think, most of all, I value how they have learned to love themselves. Those are the biggest, brightest love stories of all. They are carving out lives, five vastly different lives, that work *for* them rather than against them and allow them to be their truest selves, which is revolutionary to me. Because loving yourself in a world that measures you by what you can't do is a radical act.

And having spent so many years cloaked in shame, I am more than ready to celebrate what it is to be autistic. Shame is a leech, bloated and sick with everything it has taken from me. It is not as though I am now shame-free, but there has been progress. I used to bury my shame, and I used to be turned off by other people's shame as well. I didn't want to be near it in case I was tainted by association, or in case it was catching. But now I am drawn to talking about it, to bringing it into the light, to sharing the load. At least it is in the room now, not rattling the windows and whispering threats through the keyhole. I do wonder if shame is the natural by-product of living in a world where the dominant way of being, the most common type of thinking, is not mine. If I had grown up alone in a cabin in the woods, I wonder, would I feel any shame? There is no point in dwelling on the imaginary cabin in the woods, though – more valuable is the question of whether shame can ever be fully replaced by pride. If not in myself, maybe in the next generation. Maybe in my daughter. Maybe in her friends and family and community. I do not want shame to be her inheritance. I would much rather pride take its place.

It is confusing when people view pride as fundamentally opposed to disability, as though the concept is whitewashing hardship or plastering over pain. Pride does not seek to hide the difficult parts, only to make space for the unique goodness to be showcased as well. Celebrating what we do well does not imply there are no struggles.

I have never felt more at home than I do around other autistic people. I hope that, in reading these stories, you have felt at home too. At home in knowing there are many different ways to live a life, and the best way to ensure success for autistic people, however they wish to measure that, is through support, understanding, accommodations, connection, and love.

ACKNOWLEDGEMENTS

The logical place to start with my long list of thanks is with Chloë, Jess, Michael, Noor and Tim. Thank you. Without you this book does not exist. Thank you for your vulnerability, your time (hours and hours and hours of it), your energy, your expertise and your willingness to dive back into the hard times in the hope they will be of benefit to someone else. It has been an immeasurable privilege to be invited into your lives. Thank you for teaching me so much, for making me laugh, for making me think and for making me feel proud of what it is to be autistic.

Thank you to the additional autistic voices included in these pages – Holly, Kristy, Jen, Helen, Anna, Emmett, Felix, Jordan, Flynn, Emmie, Amelia, and Aggie. You are magnificent and I feel so lucky to include your words in this book.

Thank you to Peta and everyone at Amaze. You do such incredible work, putting autistic voices at the forefront of everything you do, and providing services and resources that genuinely make the lives of autistic people and our families better.

Thank you to Sarah Chan and Chris Varney, for your time and involvement as well.

Thank you to my publisher, Alex Lloyd. Thank you for wanting more from the discourse around love and autism, and thank you for believing in this project before I was even quite sure what it would become. To Belinda Huang and the team at Pan Macmillan, thank you for all the work you put in as *Love & Autism* went from undercooked first draft to fully formed book. Thank you Alissa Dinallo for the gorgeous cover.

Always and forever, thank you to my agent Danielle Binks for going above and beyond in your advocacy and support for me as an autistic author. You absolutely walk the talk. And to the whole team at Jacinta di Mase Management – being on your books still feels a bit like a dream.

Thank you to my family and friends for all the support with this one. It was big. You kept me going. Aggie and Arth, I love you both so much.

And for my Granda Frank, whose light, I hope, is reflected in everything I do.

This book was written on the unceded lands of the Gubbi Gubbi/ Kabbi Kabbi people.

A COMPREHENSIVE BUT INCOMPLETE READING LIST

These are the non-fiction books by autistic writers that I have read and can recommend. I have learned something about the autistic experience from each and every one. The list is incomplete, of course, but I hope this can be a starting point for anyone who wants to read more. In compiling this list, I have kept the disability rights movement phrase 'Nothing about us without us' in mind.

- *Back From The Brink: Stories of Resilience, Reconciliation and Reconnection*, Tim Chan and Sarah Chan
- *Late Bloomer: How an Autism Diagnosis Changed my Life*, Clem Bastow
- *We're Not Broken: Changing the Autism Conversation*, Eric Garcia

- *Neurotribes: The Legacy of Autism and the Future of Neuro-diversity*, Steve Silberman
- *Different, Not Less: A Neurodivergent's Guide to Embracing Your True Self and Finding Your Happily Ever After*, Chloë Hayden
- *Ten Steps To Nanette*, Hannah Gadsby
- *The Ninth Life of a Diamond Miner: A Memoir*, Grace Tame
- *Unmasking Autism: The Power of Embracing Our Hidden Neurodiversity*, Devon Price
- *The Reason I Jump: The Inner Voice of a Thirteen-Year-Old Boy with Autism*, Naoki Higashida
- *I Overcame My Autism and All I Got Was This Lousy Anxiety Disorder*, Sarah Kurchak
- *The Awesome Autistic Go-To Guide: A Practical Handbook for Autistic Teens and Tweens*, Yenn Purkis and Tanya Masterman
- *All The Weight of Our Dreams: On Living Racialized Autism*, edited by Lydia X.Z. Brown, E. Ashkenazy, and Morénike Giwa Onaiwu
- *Sincerely, Your Autistic Child: What People on the Autism Spectrum Wish Their Parents Knew about Growing Up, Acceptance, and Identity*, edited by Emily Paige Ballou, Sharon daVanport and Morénike Giwa Onaiwu
- *The Spectrum Girl's Survival Guide: How to Grow Up Awesome and Autistic*, Siena Castellon

Bibliography

Neurodiversity as natural variation: den Houting, J., 'Why Everything You Know about Autism is Wrong', TEDx Talk, November 2019.

Double empathy problem: Crompton, C.J., DeBrabander, K. et al., 'Double empathy: why autistic people are often misunderstood', *Frontiers for Young Minds*, 11 May 2021; Milton, D.E.M., 'On the ontological status of autism: the "double empathy problem"', *Disability & Society* 27 (6), 2012.

Autistic people and special interests: Grove, R., Hoekstra, R.A. et al., 'Special interests and subjective wellbeing in autistic adults', *Autism Research* 11 (5), 2018.

Autistic people meeting the criteria for ADHD: Rommelse, N.N., Franke, B. et al., 'Shared heritability of attention-deficit/hyperactivity disorder and autism spectrum disorder', *European Child & Adolescent Psychiatry* 19 (3), 2010.

Children with dyslexia 100 times more likely to receive a diagnosis than those with dyscalculia: Morsanyi, K., 'Dyscalculia: "maths dyslexia" or why so many children struggle with numbers', *The Conversation*, January 2019.

Stereotypes of autism: Draaisma, D., 'Stereotypes of autism', *Philosophical Transactions of the Royal Society of London, Series B, Biological Science* 27; 364 (1522), 2009.

The Coke can effect: Swan, V., 'This is why some kids on the autism spectrum can have meltdowns after their school day', *The Mighty*, June 2018. themighty.com

25–30 per cent of diagnosed autistic people will never develop spoken language: Anderson, D.K., Lord, C. et al., 'Patterns of growth in verbal abilities among children with autism spectrum disorder', *Journal of Consulting and Clinical Psychology* 75 (4), 2007.

Suicide rate for autistic people is three times higher than non-autistic people: Kõlves, K., Fitzgerald, C. et al., 'Assessment of suicidal behaviors among individuals with autism spectrum disorder in Denmark', *JAMA Network* 4 (1), 2021.

Suicidal behaviour in teens and young adults: Hannon, G., Taylor, E.P., 'Suicidal behaviour in adolescents and young adults with ASD: findings from a systematic review', *Clinical Psychology Review* 33 (8), 2013.

Autistic young people are more likely to be bullied than non-autistic classmates: Maïano, C., Normand, C.L. et al., 'Prevalence of school bullying among youth with autism spectrum disorders: a systematic review and meta-analysis', *Autism Research* 9, 2016.

Bullying is more likely to occur in high school: Käld, E., Beckman, L. et al., 'Exploring potential modifiers of the association between neurodevelopmental disorders and risk of bullying exposure', *JAMA Pediatrics* 176 (9), 2022.

Autism and gaming: Amaze, 'Video games and autism: helpful or harmful?' 2018. amaze.org.au

Autistic girls and women experience distinct issues relating to menstruation: Steward, R., Crane, L. et al., '"Life is much more difficult to manage during periods": autistic experiences of menstruation', *Journal of Autism and Developmental Disorders* 48 (12), 2018.

Gender diversity: Warrier, V., Greenberg, D.M. et al., 'Elevated rates of autism, other neurodevelopmental and psychiatric diagnoses, and autistic traits in transgender and gender-diverse individuals', *Nature Communications* 11 (1), 2020.

Autistic students more likely to be suspended from school: Bowden, N., Gibb, S. et al., 'Association between high-need education-based funding and school suspension rates for autistic students in New Zealand', *JAMA Pediatrics*, 2022.

Amaze report on unemployment rate for autistic people: Jones, S., Muhammad, A. et al., 'Autism and employment in Australia', 2019. amaze.org.au

Autism represented as a childhood disability: Stevenson, J.L., Harp, B. et al., 'Infantilizing autism', *Disability Studies Quarterly* 31 (3), 2011.

Loneliness in autistic adults: Mazurek, M.O., 'Loneliness, friendship, and well-being in adults with autism spectrum disorders', *Autism* 18 (3), 2014.

Acceptance of autism reduces loneliness: Umagami, K., Remington, A. et al., 'Loneliness in autistic adults: a systematic review', *Autism* 26 (8), 2022.

Autistic children are 160 times more likely to drown than non-autistic children: Guan, J., Li, G., 'Injury mortality in individuals with autism', *American Journal of Public Health* 107 (5), 2017.

Animal-assisted therapy: O'Haire, M., 'Research on animal-assisted intervention and autism spectrum disorder, 2012–2015', *Applied Developmental Science* 21 (3), 2017.

Autism as inspiration porn: Young, S., 'We're not here for your inspiration', *ABC The Drum*, 2012.

Autism and pregnancy: Kerr, K., 'Going through childbirth when you're autistic', *SBS Voices*, 2021.

Autism and pain: Failla, M.D., Gerdes, M.B. et al., 'Increased pain sensitivity and pain-related anxiety in individuals with autism', *PAIN Reports* 16; 5 (6), 2020.

Executive functioning: Demetriou, E.A., DeMayo, M.M. et al., 'Executive function in autism spectrum disorder: history, theoretical models, empirical findings, and potential as an endophenotype', *Frontiers in Psychiatry* 10 (753), 2019.

Autistic people and the impact of the pandemic: Oomen, D., Nijhof, A.D. et al., 'The psychological impact of the COVID-19 pandemic on adults with autism: a survey study across three countries', *Molecular Autism* 12, 21, 2021.

Autism and Ramadan: Abdul, N., 'My daughter and I are both autistic. This is how we do Ramadan', *SBS Voices*, 2021.